QUILTING

SIMPLIFIED

Fresh Designs and Easy
Instructions for Beginners

Choly Knight

QUILTING SIMPLIFIED

Fresh Designs and Easy
Instructions for Beginn

Choly Knight

Acquisition editor: **Peg Couch**

Cover and layout designer:
Ashley Millhouse

Developmental editor: **Nathalie Mornu**

Editor: **Katie Weeber**

Project photography: **Eric Forberger**

Step-by-step photography:
Matthew McClure

ISBN 978-1-57421-902-9

Library of Congress Cataloging-in-Publication Data

Knight, Choly.
 Quilting simplified : fresh designs and easy instructions for beginners / Choly Knight.
   pages cm
 Includes index.
 ISBN 978-1-57421-902-9
 1. Patchwork quilts. 2. Patchwork--Patterns. 3. Quilting--Patterns. I. Title.
 TT835.K564 2015
 746.46--dc23
                     2014041285

Printed in China
First printing

About the Author

Choly Knight is from Orlando, Florida, and is the author of *Sew Kawaii!, Sew Baby, Sewing Stylish Handbags & Totes, Sew Me! Sewing Basics, Sew Me! Sewing Home Décor, Bling It Up!, Awesome Duct Tape Projects,* and *Craft Projects for Minecraft® and Pixel Art Fans.* She has been crafting for as long as she can remember, and has drawn, painted, sculpted, and stitched everything in sight. She began sewing clothing in 1997 and has yet to put her sewing machine away. After studying studio art and earning a BA in English, she now enjoys trying to find numerous different ways to combine her passions for writing, fine art, and craft art. She created all of the designs, projects, and patterns that appear in this book. She focuses on handcrafted clothing, accessories, and other creations inspired by Japanese art, anime, and style, and specializes in cosplay (costume play) hats and hoodies. You can find out more about her and her work on her website: *www.cholyknight.com.*

Contents

The Quilts! 62

Build Your Skills:

❏ Learn about the tools

❏ Understand fabric cuts, selection, and anatomy

❏ Choose your palette

❏ Prepare your fabric

❏ Understand quilt anatomy

❏ Basic piecing

❏ Foundation piecing

❏ Fusible web appliqué

❏ Freezer paper appliqué

❏ Planning your quilt back

❏ Making the quilt sandwich

❏ Quilt tying

❏ Machine quilting

❏ Quilt-as-you-go quilting

❏ Binding

Introduction

My first quilt was made primarily out of necessity, but I never imagined how addicted I would become. I started sewing by making my own clothes and accessories, and anyone who sews will tell you how quick and easy it is to amass a huge stash of fabric scraps after only a few projects. I had squirreled away an unmanageable trove of material beneath my bed, and I tried every trick up my sleeve to get rid of it: gift purses for friends, matching hats for all my outfits, and every other trinket made from fabric you can imagine.

But I was ignoring the elephant in the room—quilts. I learned from sewing books that a quilt is the quintessential scrap-busting project, used for that very purpose from the onset of sewing history. But I was convinced that quilting was way beyond my ability—it seemed like an art only practiced by skilled masters who could sew precise ¼" (6mm) seams without even looking and used an arsenal of templates, rulers, and guides for even the most basic projects. I felt I couldn't even think about quilting until I was a veteran sewer. Meanwhile, my closets were quickly filling with scraps and I was drowning in fabric.

I decided I had to sew myself out of the fabric pile I had created. I didn't have many of the fancy templates and tools that dedicated quilters do, but I studied to find shortcuts, tricks, and techniques that allowed me to make the quilt I wanted without so many hard and fast rules.

Even though my first quilt was unusual, to say the least—made from an eclectic mix of satins, denim, and cotton with more than a handful of wonky seams and frayed edges—I was surprised by how much I loved the process. I found it breathtaking watching a tiny swatch of fabric slowly grow into a massive quilt top through all that piecing. And I loved how quilting turned a random pile of fabric into an intricate collage with so much depth and texture. I was immediately hooked.

> "I loved how quilting turned a random pile of fabric into an intricate collage with so much depth and texture."

I hope that when you start to see the quilting possibilities ahead of you, you'll become hooked, too. Creating a full quilt will likely be one of the biggest sewing endeavors you tackle, taking weeks or even months, but I think you'll find it's worth it for the immense payoff you receive. Not only will your quilt be a unique handmade item that will last for years, but it's also something like a time capsule. Quilts are a beautiful way of showcasing a collection of favorite fabrics and motifs that you fell in love with at that particular time.

Because taking the plunge into quilting can be intimidating, in this book I'll teach you everything I know about making the process as easy as possible. You'll find uncommon and underrated techniques that make quilting approachable and foolproof. Once you're comfortable, use the techniques to dive into making your first quilt project!

Whether you're fresh-faced and ready to try patchwork for the first time or completely comfortable with quilting and need some modern inspiration, I'm sure you'll find something new to learn from this book!

Why Quilting Can Seem Daunting, and Why It Doesn't Have to Be

I've come across many other sewers who are intimidated to attempt a full-fledged quilt, and I've been there myself. A quilt will be a little more costly and time-intensive than other sewing projects, but it doesn't need to feel so overwhelming if you keep the right attitude.

Cost. Keep it simple: Designer, high-quality fabrics are a treat to work with, but a little pricey. If you're making something large, or not sure what you'll design just yet, consider buying solid colors of your favorite brands. They're often much cheaper than their printed counterparts and are a fun way to experiment.

Time. Break it up: An incredibly large or intricate quilt can take weeks or even months to complete. But if you take it one block or one row at time, you can enjoy the journey and focus without getting overwhelmed.

Process. Take the scenic route: The guidelines and techniques in this book are just that—guidelines, best practice methods to ensure you end up happy with your project. There will always be new ways to build a quilt, and maybe you'll be the one to find them! Unless you plan to enter a quilt show or expect your creation to stay pristine for centuries, have a little fun, go against the grain, and try something new.

Fresh Designs in Quilting

It's so easy to make fresh, modern quilts to suit your taste. Start with the overall look. You can alter a more traditional design to a sleek and bold aesthetic, using bright, saturated colors in contrast with the cool neutrals gray and white. Try some large and graphic designs, perhaps something geometric, with big expanses of negative space.

Beyond that, don't be afraid to break some of the more traditional rules and find new paths. You can simplify the process by using some non-traditional methods that make quilting faster and easier. I think an attitude of experimentation, improvisation, and bold, simple design is perfect for budding quilters. If you feel at all apprehensive about getting started, this book will be your gentle reminder to keep trying new things, making mistakes, and celebrating the simple things you get right rather than worrying over what you get wrong.

The projects in this book totally embrace a clean, bold aesthetic, but they're all assembled using surprisingly simple methods. The end result will be stunning and modern, but you'll find the construction is completely achievable. Here are some additional great-looking quilts that are surprisingly simple to make. Check out these pages and get inspired to dive in and make a quilt that you love!

Bottom: Modern quilted potholders by Emily Tarsha, *www.simplynotable.com*.

Left: Reverse Hopscotch quilt by Vanessa Christenson, *www.vandco.bigcartel.com*.

Opposite page: Oodalolly quilt by Rachel Hauser, *www.stitchedincolor.com*.

Below: Indelible Pow Wow quilt by Svetlana Sotak, *www.sotakhandmade.blogspot.com.*

Left: A Modern Table Runner by Nicole Neblett, *www.mamalovequilts.blogspot.com*

Going Circular pillows by Katie Pedersen, *www.sewkatiedid.wordpress.com.*

Machine stitched
hexagons by
Nicole Daksiewicz,
*www.modern-
handcraft.com*.

Getting Started

If you've never quilted before, this is the place to start! Preparing to quilt might seem like a daunting task, but in truth, you don't need a whole lot to get started. This book describes the most basic of tools and techniques that will open a wealth of possibilities, and you won't get bogged down with extra gadgets and rules you don't need to know just yet. Take note of this section during your next shopping trip so you'll know exactly what to look for!

The Hardware: Essential Quilting Tools

The first time you venture into the quilting tools section of your local fabric store, you might be surprised to find that there's a quilting tool for practically every style of quilt out there. The truth is, you only need a few select tools to get the ball rolling. (You can treat yourself to the fancy gadgets later!) These are the most basic quilting tools to get you started, and ones you'll use for the lifetime of your quilting pursuit, so treat them well and look forward to all the fun you'll get to have with them!

Sewing machine: If you're looking into buying a new machine for quilting, know that a reliable mechanical machine with only a straight and zigzag stitch can make just about any kind of quilt. So yes, you can use your regular sewing machine if you already have one. But if you're in the market to buy a machine and a fancy model has caught your eye, consider the features you want before pulling out your wallet. These are all options that can make quilting easier, but are not required. And many of these features are

available on sewing machines not designed for quilting, so again, a regular mechanical machine will serve you just fine to get started.

- **Adjustable feed dogs:** Just about every quilting machine will come with this feature, but not all general sewing machines will. In order to do free-motion quilting (page 54), you'll need to drop the feed dogs in your machine so that you're free to move the quilt around without the machine trying to move it for you.

Quilting sewing machine. These machines will look much the same as typical sewing machines, but with some added features to make quilting a bit easier. The extended table is usually a dead giveaway. Don't feel like you have to run out and buy one of these to make a quilt—your regular home sewing machine is definitely enough to get you started.

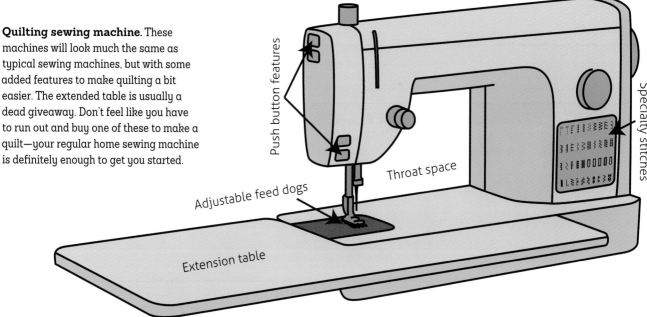

Push button features

Specialty stitches

Throat space

Adjustable feed dogs

Extension table

TIP

If you're finding the shopping process too overwhelming, consider shopping at a quilting store instead of a fabric shop. You won't get bogged down by non-quilting items, and the employees there can help you every step of the way!

Walking foot. Also called an even-feed foot, this foot takes an extra bit of installation, but it's worth the effort. It simulates a second set of feed dogs going above the fabric, ensuring that all layers of your quilt run through the machine at the same rate.

Piecing foot (optional). A piecing foot (also called a patchwork foot or ¼" foot), has a distinctive ridge that extends on the side of the foot. You can butt your seams against this while you sew for better accuracy.

Darning foot (optional). Also called an embroidery foot. The open needle area and spring-powered pressure allow you to move your project freehand while you sew. It offers just enough pressure to hold on to your work without giving any resistance.

- **Throat space:** Most quilting sewing machines have a larger area between the needle and side panel than general machines. This gives you more room to work with your quilt while machine quilting. If you plan to do your own machine quilting (see page 52) in the future, you should definitely look for this option.

- **Extension table:** The second most common feature in quilting sewing machines is an extension table. These typically snap onto your machine to give you a large flat space to the left of the machine on which to rest your quilt while you piece or machine quilt. This makes machine quilting a bit easier, but not nearly as much as extra throat space does.

- **Walking foot:** There are lots of specialty feet you can purchase for your machine, but this is only one you'll really need to do your own quilting. Also called an even-feed foot, this machine foot enables you to machine quilt your quilt layers without worry of puckers or wrinkles caused by one layer of the quilt feeding through the machine at a different rate than

the others. Some quilting sewing machines have this built in, but you can just as easily purchase this foot separately.

- **Piecing foot:** Specialty sewing machines often come with extra sewing machine feet that perform interesting functions. One of these is a piecing foot. It has a ridge that extends precisely ¼" (6mm) out from your needle position, resulting in a ¼" (6mm) seam every time you sew with it. It's not a necessity (see page 38 for alternatives), but it really makes piecing foolproof. Note that you can purchase this foot separately—it doesn't have to come bundled with a new machine.

- **Darning foot:** Also called an embroidery foot, this presser foot enables you to do free-motion quilting. In conjunction with lowering your feed dogs, this foot allows you to quilt your project by moving the quilt freehand beneath the needle without the machine pulling the fabric through. This means you can go in any direction and, with some practice, create lots of intricate designs.

- **Specialty stitches:** Decorative stitches are a very common feature of high-end machines, often reaching hundreds of options with some models. I personally prefer large, less dainty forms of embellishment. If considering this option, you should think about your desired finished result before you become infatuated with the surplus of stitches available on specialty machines. Do most of your quilt project plans involve intricate decorative stitches, or are you working toward a more clean and simple look? Tiny embellishing stitches are fun for some creations, but I don't think you'll end up using them in most quilting projects.

- **Push button features:** Do mundane tasks like lowering your presser foot, lowering or raising your needle, cutting threads, or threading your needle slow you down? If these little chores really irritate you, you'll be happy to know many high-end quilting machines have push button features to take care of them for you. It raises the price tag, but if that convenience saves you loads of frustration, you might consider it!

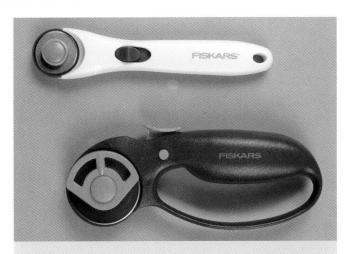

Rotary cutters. This tool is like an extremely sharp pizza cutter for fabric. Used in conjunction with a cutting mat and ruler, it ensures extremely consistent and accurate straight cuts.

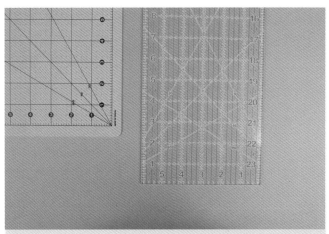

Ruler and cutting mat. A quilting ruler (at right) allows you to accurately measure and cut rectangles and various angles, while a cutting mat (at left) absorbs the nicks from your cutting blade. You will frequently work with them together.

Rotary cutter: As a quilter, you'll mostly be doing straight-line fabric cutting. While regular sewing shears can accomplish this just fine, the most efficient way to make straight cuts is with a rotary cutter. It works just like a pizza cutter, but is far sharper for cutting fabric. For best results, you'll need to use it in conjunction with a ruler and cutting mat. For safety, be sure to use the safety latch and replace the blade as soon as it becomes dull (usually after three quilts or so). Rotary cutters come as small as 18mm in diameter and as large as 60mm; smaller sizes work nicely for intricate curved cuts, while larger sizes are best for simple straight cuts. To get started, try a 45mm or 60mm size (depending on which feels more comfortable in your hand) and consider getting more sizes as your skills progress. See page 34 to learn how to use this tool properly.

THE QUILTER'S TOOLKIT

The tool lists in this book mention a quilter's toolkit. These basic supplies are required for every project. Refer to this list to see what you need.

- ☐ Sewing machine
- ☐ Rotary cutter
- ☐ Quilting ruler
- ☐ Cutting mat
- ☐ Sewing shears
- ☐ Crafting scissors
- ☐ Iron & ironing board
- ☐ Sewing machine needles
- ☐ Sewing pins
- ☐ Seam ripper
- ☐ Fabric marker/pencil
- ☐ Basting glue
- ☐ Organizational tools: plastic bags, sticky notes, etc.

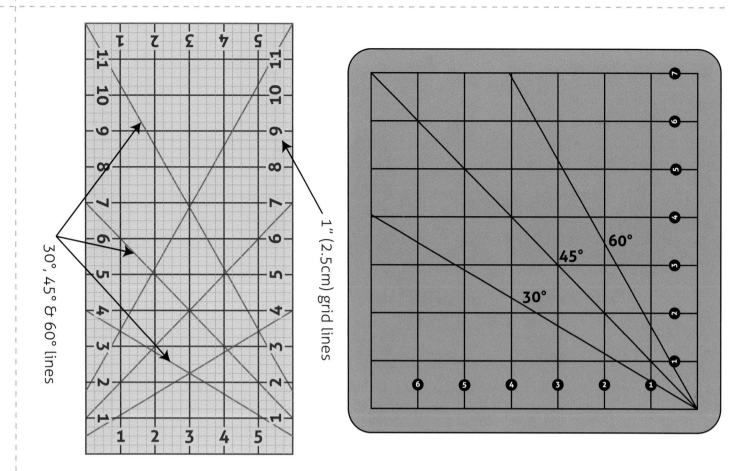

30°, 45° & 60° lines

1" (2.5cm) grid lines

30°

45°

60°

- **Quilting ruler:** The word ruler might cause you to visualize the simple wooden one from elementary school, but quilting rulers are an entirely different animal. They're square or rectangular in shape, transparent, and have a grid printed over the entire surface, allowing you to measure squares and strips in a flash. You'll use this as a guide, running your rotary cutter against it to churn out quilting pieces in no time at all. (Note that rulers come marked with either inches or metric measurements, but you should never mix them on the same project.) A simple 12" x 6" (30 x 15cm) ruler is usually enough to get started, but you might consider getting a 24" (60cm)-long ruler (along with some other smaller rulers for detail work) as you build your repertoire. Be sure to look for rulers with ¼" (6mm) grid lines; a 30-, 45-, and 60-degree line is an added plus.

- **Cutting mat:** This last crucial part of your cutting trio should have a grid printed on it, just like your quilting ruler. (Some even come with inches on one side and metrics on the other.) The mat is made out of a material that can stand up to the abuse caused by your ultra-sharp rotary cutter blade. When cutting, you'll rest your fabric and ruler on this mat; it absorbs all the cutting damage so your table doesn't have to! You can also use the grid guides in tandem with your quilting ruler to get the most accurate measurements. Large mats (such as 24" x 36" [61 x 92cm]) are easier to work on, but you won't want a mat that's larger than your worktable. If it's a better fit, a smaller 18" x 24" (45 x 60cm) mat will work just as well.

- **Sewing shears:** While most of your fabric cutting will be done with a rotary cutter, sewing shears are still a staple of the quilting workspace, as you'll need them for cutting curved shapes in fabric. Even a cheap pair of sewing shears will cut better than regular utility scissors, especially if you treat them right and only use them on fabric. Paper, thread, and other materials can quickly dull the edge of a pair of shears.

- **Crafting scissors:** For all of your non-fabric cutting needs, be they templates, paper patterns, or thread, a simple pair of comfortable crafting scissors will do the trick.

- **Iron & ironing board:** Pressing your sewn seams as you work is crucial to achieving good quilting results. A basic iron and ironing board work just fine, but make sure both items are clean and in good working order. Spritzing clean water from a spray bottle onto your fabric just before pressing can also help steam your seams flat.

- **Sewing machine needles:** Universal sewing needles are okay to use for a quick project, but long-term piecing will go better with quilting needles in the 70/10–80/12 range. Machine quilting will require some heavier needles—ranging up to 90/14 or more if you find needle breakage to be a problem. Also consider Microtex machine needles. These have a super thin, acute point, which produces more accurate stitches for techniques like topstitching. Be sure to replace your needle when it starts to get dull—after every quilt or so.

- **Sewing pins:** These temporarily hold your fabric pieces together while you're in the process of sewing them. Long, sharp pins work best for quilting, especially ones with flat heads that lie flush against the fabric while you sew or iron.

- **Basting glue:** As an alternative to sewing pins, basting glue works to temporarily hold your fabric together while you sew. It's more precise than pins, less cumbersome, and washes out with water. It isn't reusable like sewing pins, though, so it's best saved for cases when it's especially helpful, such as for paper foundation piecing and some appliqué.

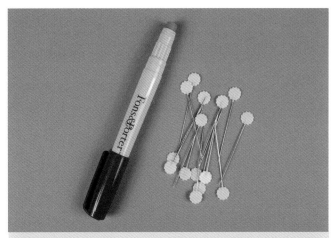

Pins and glue. Options for holding your fabric together while you sew include pins and basting glue. While pins with round heads will work, those with flat heads are most convenient because they lie flat against your fabric while you work. Basting glue is a nice alternative for hard-to-reach areas.

- **Seam ripper:** Just like with any other kind of project, mistakes can happen, and this little tool will take care of ripping out stitches without damaging your fabric. Don't be afraid to use it, as going back and fixing a little error is better than starting all over.

- **Fabric marker:** It might not seem like it, but the ability to make little marks on your fabric can do wonders to help with assembly. You can use a fabric marker where pins fall short to match up areas that need to be sewn precisely. A dark water- or air-soluble marker works best on light fabrics, while a light pencil or tailor's chalk works nicely on dark fabrics.

- **Organization:** Quilting can involve working with lots of little pieces at one time, so if you're the type who prefers to keep things tidy, consider investing in some organizing supplies, such as plastic bags, boxes, and sticky notes for your stacks of fabric pieces. You can label and bundle fabric bits while they're not in use, and you'll be sure they're ready for you the next time you sit down to sew.

Quilting Simplified

21

The Software: Quilting Materials

Once you have all the necessary tools, the second half of your shopping adventure involves gathering your quilting materials. This is all the soft stuff you'll use in conjunction with your handy new tools. Items like fabric and batting will reflect your own personal style, as you get to select the color, texture, and overall feel. Here I'll provide some tips to help you make your choices so you wind up happy with your purchases.

Fabric

Choosing fabric for your quilt is a whole process unto itself; in fact, full books have been written on the subject. It's akin to picking the paint colors for an entire painting, so it can seem complicated. But there are tricks and shortcuts you can use to avoid becoming overwhelmed. For now, I say pick fabrics that will net you the most fun, and save some of the more complicated elements of fabric selection for when you're a seasoned quilter!

The old standbys

After quilting cotton, the rest of the fabrics here are virtually interchangeable. They will have their own quirks and characteristics, but for the most part will behave like quilting cotton, just with less durability over time.

100% quilting cotton: Quilting cotton, sometimes called calico or broadcloth, is the go-to fabric for quilting because of its dense weave of fibers. It stands up to all of the needle piercing, plus the ironing and washing quilts usually endure for many years—and it will get softer over time to boot. It comes in a wealth of colors and patterns and is usually stiff and sturdy thanks to the dense weave and the layers of ink used to make those cheerful designs. When you visit a dedicated quilting shop, you will likely find only 100% quilting cotton there. If you want to start your project with the most user-friendly fabric available, quilting cotton is the way to go.

QUILT BACKING

The back of your quilt (see page 35 for the anatomy of a quilt) should typically be made from quilting cotton or a sturdy material similar to the front of your quilt. If you're making a particularly large quilt, you might have to piece the quilt back (see page 48), but keep an eye out for extra-wide quilt backing fabric while shopping. It's typically available in broadcloth and flannel. The colors and designs are often limited, but you never know when one might match your design perfectly.

Quilting cotton. 100% quilting cotton, with its dense weave and bright patterns, is perfectly suited for making quilts that will last for generations. You'll find it in prints of different sizes and colors, as well as solids.

Flannel: Like a plushy cousin of quilting cotton, flannel is just as stable, but with some added fuzziness and loft. It does tend to pill and unravels a little more easily than quilting cotton, but it's wonderfully cozy, and the colors available are particularly suitable for babies and kids.

Flannel. A much softer and warmer alternative to quilting cotton, flannel isn't quite as hard-wearing, but it's still just as easy to work with.

Linen. Though prone to raveling, linen has a distinctive old-world charm that lends itself well to small patchwork projects.

Linen: One hundred percent linen and linen cotton blends have a wonderful homey, earthy quality that looks beautiful in home décor projects. Working with linen requires extra care, however, because the threads tend to unravel very easily.

Unconventional fabrics

Some quilters get started because they dream of creating a quilt from old clothes—perhaps favorite old t-shirts or items left to them by a beloved family member. Experts say that beginners should steer clear of any fabric other than quilting cotton, but this book is about modern quilting, which means bending the rules! It's possible to make patchwork pieces from other fabrics—you'll just have to change your technique a bit. Methods like increasing your seam allowance, foundation piecing (page 40), tying your quilt (page 51), or simply choosing a pattern with larger patchwork pieces will increase your chances of success. Unconventional quilting fabrics will throw you some curveballs now and again, so all in all it's best to have lots of fool-proof techniques at your disposal when using them.

Felt: Felt is kind of in a class all its own; it's made from pressed wool fibers and doesn't fray like typical quilting fabrics. This makes it perfect for embellishments like appliqué, but it's also suitable for any patchwork with large pieces. Try to steer clear of acrylic or polyester felts, as they don't behave nearly as well as their all-natural wool counterpart.

Corduroy: Corduroy blends the softness of flannel with the sophistication of linen. Thin wale varieties are perfect for quilting, as they aren't too thick and can handle lots of patchwork. Medium wale varieties also work well, but will require larger seam allowances and patchwork sizes.

Corduroy. Corduroy is a winning combination of sturdy and soft. Because it's a little thicker than other fabrics, it's best suited for large patchwork or patchwork where accuracy isn't an issue.

Fleece: This plush fabric might not seem like a good fit for quilts, but in some cases it works really well! For instance, fleece can often be used as a replacement for quilt batting or for patchwork projects with large pieces. Wearable items and baby items look especially nice with the color choices available.

Velvet: Sort of like the luxurious cousin of corduroy, velvet is extremely soft, but requires some special care to sew. It behaves better with large seam allowances and patchwork pieces. Foundation piecing (page 40) helps the most when working with velvet, because the fabric tends to shift while you sew it. Ironing may also be tricky; you can iron velvet carefully by placing it face down on a towel and using a press cloth. Or simply throw caution to the wind and use the iron directly on the fabric (set to a low temperature); you'll just end up with crushed velvet instead—not a bad payoff! For more inspiration, do some research on Victorian crazy quilts, where you'll often encounter velvet and satin fabrics.

Satin: While probably the most finicky of the unconventional fabrics, satin can be tamed using foundation piecing (page 40) and large seam allowances. Brocades tend to be sturdier than other satins, but they all fray quite a bit and have a delicate weave. Don't go too heavy on the quilting (quilt tying is a better option), because satin can't stand up to hard wear. Satins also work well as accents, used in conjunction with more stable fabrics like corduroy or quilting cotton.

What to avoid

Some fabrics are more trouble than they are worth when it comes to quilting. These include thin stretchy fabrics like jersey or Lycra; heavy, stiff fabrics like canvas; and anything heavily ornamented or embroidered like jacquard.

Felt. Because it's thick and won't fray, felt is often used as an embellishment and in small patchwork. Vintage wool felt is particularly popular for making incredibly warm classic quilts.

How quilting cottons are sold

You will most commonly find fabrics in the store rolled up on bolts. The fabric is then cut from the bolt in the yardage you need (usually in increments of ⅛ yd. (10cm) by your friendly fabric shop employee. The fabric on the bolt can range from 42"–44" (105–112cm) wide and 8–10 yd. (8–10m) long. The materials list for your selected pattern will tell you how many yards to buy. But that's not the only way quilting fabrics are sold.

Fat quarters: The second most common fabric cut seen in fabric stores is the fat quarter. These are often sold neatly wrapped and folded, allowing you to grab a large variety without a trip to the cutting counter. Fat quarters are available in both the metric and the English measurement system (the one that uses inches and yards and is most common in the United States), but their dimensions will be different.

In the English system, a regular ¼ yd. (roughly 23cm) cut of fabric measures 9" x 42" (about 23 x 106.5cm), but a fat quarter is cut from the corner of 1 yd. (91.5cm) of fabric, creating a piece that's 18" x 21" (about 45.5 x 53.5cm). Metric fat quarters are also cut from the corner of the fabric, but in this case from 1 meter of cloth, so they measure 50 x 55cm (roughly 19½ x 21½ inches).

Fat quarters allow you to cut wider squares and other shapes from the fabric than a narrower regular quarter of a yard (or quarter of a meter) strip would allow.

Fat eighths: Not as common as fat quarters, fat eighths are also cut along the width of the fabric, resulting in a wider 9" x 21" (23 x 53.5cm) square. (They measure 50 x 27cm in the metric system.)

Precut squares: Also known as charm squares or layer cakes, precut squares are bundles of fabric squares ranging from 5" x 5" (12.5 x 12.5cm) to 10" x 10" (25.5 x 25.5cm). These are perfect if you want to make a quilt with a small repeating block that varies in color throughout.

Precut strips: Sometimes known as jelly rolls or honey buns, these are strips that range from 1"–3" (2.5–7.5cm) by the width of the fabric from which they were cut. They're perfect for quilts with lots of stripes or tiny squares.

Thread

A little spool of thread might seem humble, but between piecing and quilting, your project is going to have several spools of thread holding it together by the time you finish. So be sure to get the best quality thread you can afford.

Polyester: Polyester thread is considered a universal thread that's great for all sewing projects, so there's no need to hesitate about using this synthetic material.

Cotton: Cotton thread is a great choice for purists who prefer to make quilts of heirloom quality. Steer clear of hand-quilting thread for piecing, as this thread has a waxy coating that won't play well with your machine.

After you've selected the type of thread you'd like to use, the question of color is really quite easy. Simply choose a neutral color that blends in nicely with all of your fabrics and is unlikely to stand out amidst your patchwork. Shades of gray work well with cool color schemes, while beige blends in nicely with warm color schemes (see page 29 for more about color schemes).

Thread. Because quilts include so many colors at once, it's much simpler to pick out a high-quality thread in a neutral color that blends nicely with all your fabrics. Pick a bright color if your quilt is monochromatic.

Batting

Batting is the fluffy layer placed between the quilt top and quilt bottom. It's usually sold in precut packages that correspond to common quilt and quilt project sizes. It's also sold by the yard in widths that reach up to 120" (305cm). Double-check the measurements of your finished project so you can select batting that fits your creation perfectly. See page 50 for more information about assembling a quilt.

Cotton: Cotton batting is a dense, natural batting that's much thinner than polyester and easy to quilt through. It usually shrinks in the wash. In a finished quilt, this shrinkage typically produces a pleasant crinkly effect that most quilters love.

Fusible fleece interfacing: While technically more interfacing than batting, fusible fleece is an iron-on batting that adds stability to the fabric you adhere it to, while also adding a bit of loft. It's great for small quilting projects because you don't have to worry about basting. It also works for any other project that benefits from stability without becoming too rigid. Fusible fleece is often sold in precut squares or by the yard in widths of 45" (when sold by the meter, it comes in 90cm and 150cm widths).

Insulated batting: This batting is typically paired with projects intended for kitchen use, such as potholders and casserole covers. It reflects the temperature of the items placed inside it, keeping hot foods hot and cold foods cold. Like fusible fleece, this is also sold in precut packages or by the yard in widths of 45" (114cm).

Polyester: If you encounter a particularly puffy quilt, it probably contains polyester batting. This kind of batting tends to have a very high loft, which can make it difficult to quilt through, especially if the quilt is large. If using polyester batting, you might also encounter bearding, where the batting gathers and bunches inside the quilt, creating a tangled mess. This batting is not recommended for quilting unless you use the quilt tying method (page 51).

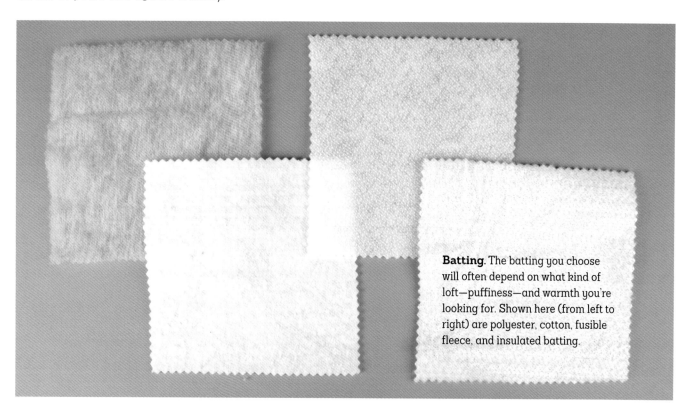

Batting. The batting you choose will often depend on what kind of loft—puffiness—and warmth you're looking for. Shown here (from left to right) are polyester, cotton, fusible fleece, and insulated batting.

Batting can be purchased in pre-cut blanket-sized rolls or by the yard. Be sure to purchase batting that is roughly 8" (20.5cm) wider and longer than your patchwork so it will end up being 4" (10cm) larger on all sides. (The larger your quilt top, the more important it is to have at least 8 inches [10cm] of play, as the batting will shrink up during the quilting process.) If purchasing by the yard, check the width of the batting to be sure that it is wider than one edge of your quilt top by 8" (20.5cm). Then ask for a yardage length equivalent to the other edge of your quilt plus 8" (20.5cm).

Calculating batting. Ideally, you should purchase a batting section big enough to cover your quilt top plus 8" (20.5cm). Batting comes bagged precut in common blanket sizes, or you can pick out a bolt of batting that matches your quilt's width and order the appropriate length.

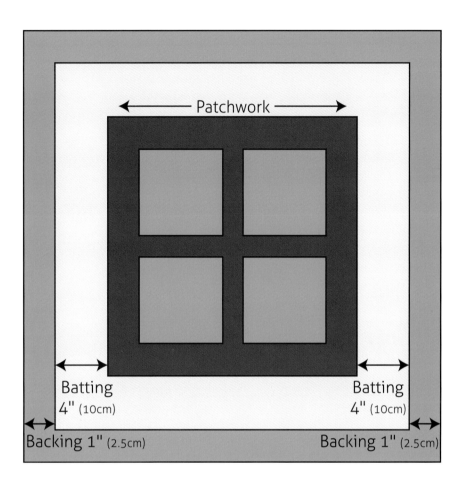

Choosing Your Palette: Quilting Color Theory

Now that you've selected the type of fabric you'd like to use, next up is choosing the colors. You can purchase a fabric bundle or collection and let the designer do the coordinating for you, or you can learn a bit about color theory and select your own colors. Either way, these tips will make the decision as easy as possible.

Coordinating precut fabrics

While fabrics for apparel and home décor are only sold off the bolt, quilting fabrics are used much like paints on a palette, so they're marketed and sold in lots of different ways. The fat quarters, fat eighths, precut squares, and precut strips described on page 26 can be found in bundles of coordinating colors, so all the matching is done for you, and they're an easy way to build up your fabric collection so it's beautiful, varied, and coordinated. Designer fabrics are often sold like this, allowing designers to show off an entire fabric collection.

Many quilt patterns will cater to these kinds of bundles, and this book is no different! Check the tip sections for each project to see how to use fabric bundles with the patterns.

Selecting a color scheme

If you'd rather choose your own color scheme than select fabric bundles that make the decision for you, there are some failsafe ways to get a fabulous-looking quilt without having to study the color wheel for ages.

Pick a star fabric: If you already have a fabric you're itching to quilt with, then you're in business! Simply use that star fabric and then choose complementary fabrics to match.

Monochromatic scheme: A really foolproof way to get a fresh and modern quilt is to go monochromatic. Choose one color that you adore and get fabrics in every shade of that color you can find. To add a fresh bit of contrast, bring in some white, gray, or black to go alongside your color as a clean background.

Complementary color scheme: If you want to take it one step further, a monochromatic color scheme with just a pop of complementary color (the color on the color wheel opposite the shade you've chosen) looks very sophisticated. Simply limit one block or section of your quilt to a complementary color and the purposeful contrast will look very artistic.

Analogous color scheme: Similar to the monochromatic color scheme, analogous colors are adjacent to each other on the color wheel. To keep it simple, limit yourself to just three or four colors and try not to vary the saturation (color intensity) too much.

Go your own way

If you decide you want to try making your own color scheme, keep the following things in mind.

Create contrast: If you want to have colors in your quilt pop out, creating a focus color versus a background color, you need to choose your background fabrics accordingly.

Hues opposite one another on the color wheel contrast the most with each other. Warm colors (red, orange, and yellow) tend to stand out, while cool colors (blue, green, and purple) tend to recede.

The color wheel. Using the color wheel as a quick guide can help you easily find beautiful matches to your favorite colors.

Colors with high value (light colors) contrast with colors of low value (dark colors), making them both stand out more when used together than they otherwise would alone.

Saturated (intense) colors stand out more than their neutral (dull) counterparts. Gray and beige, and even white and black, serve as reliable neutral backgrounds.

Scale: Fabrics with large motifs (large-scale prints) are best used for large patchwork or, even better, for the back of your quilt. When cut up into small pieces, large-scale prints lose their context. Small-scale prints, however, are best used for small patchwork. When used in large areas, the details of small-scale prints get lost and they appear like solid fabrics.

Scrap quilt coordination: Even the most ragtag group of fabrics can seem to coordinate well if they're all bordered with the same matching fabric. Use this method to get rid of fabric scraps that don't seem to mesh!

Star fabric color scheme. After finding a fabric I absolutely loved and wanted to feature in my quilt—the raccoon print shown at center—I then developed a color scheme by finding fabrics that matched the accent colors within it.

Monochromatic color scheme. Simply stick to shades of your favorite color and you've gone monochromatic!

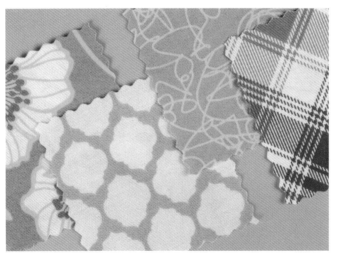

Complementary color scheme. Add a pop of a complementary color to your monochromatic scheme and get an instant "dare to be different" artsy feel.

Analogous color scheme. Pick a range of a few colors that appear next to each other on the color wheel and you'll get a harmonious blended look.

Prepping Your Fabric

Now that you've purchased all of your wonderful fabrics, there are a few things you need to do to prepare them before you dive into your first project.

Pre-washing: If you've purchased fabric yardage, pre-washing is highly recommended. It pre-shrinks the fabric so it doesn't shrink more in your finished quilt; it removes the sizing (light starch) that can be found on retail fabrics; and it also washes out excess dyes that might leech onto other fabrics in your quilt or onto your clothes as you sew. I prefer to wash in warm water and dry with a cool setting. The one downside to pre-washing is that it will cause your fabric edges to fray, wasting a bit of your fabric. For this reason, you should not pre-wash precut fabric bundles, especially strips and small squares. Otherwise, you'll end up with a bundle of snarled threads in your washing machine, and hardly any fabric at all!

Ironing: If your fabric has been pre-washed or simply has wrinkles from the store, you'll want to iron it so it's prepared for cutting. A spritz of water from a spray bottle will help steam out the wrinkles quickly.

Quilting Simplified

31

FABRIC ANATOMY

Selvedge: The outside machine-finished edge of manufactured fabric. It has a special weave and texture to it, making it different from the actual fabric yardage. It often has fabric information printed on it, such as the designer and color palette. Using the selvedges in your patchwork can lead to some complications, so it's best to trim them off.

Lengthwise grain: Also called the warp threads, this is the direction of the fabric that runs parallel to the selvedge edges. It carries the most strength and stability, as these threads don't stretch.

Crosswise grain: Also called the weft threads, this is the direction of the fabric that runs perpendicular to the selvedge edges, along the width of the fabric. These threads are slightly stretchy, but are still very stable.

Bias grain: This is the direction of the fabric that runs at an exact 45-degree diagonal between the lengthwise and crosswise grains (essentially from corner to corner of your fabric piece). Pieces cut on the bias will stretch significantly, making them useful for quilting only when curves are involved.

The most stable patchwork pieces will be cut on the straight grain, either the lengthwise or the crosswise one. Pieces cut at even a slight diagonal might stretch and cause you to end up with wonky patchwork.

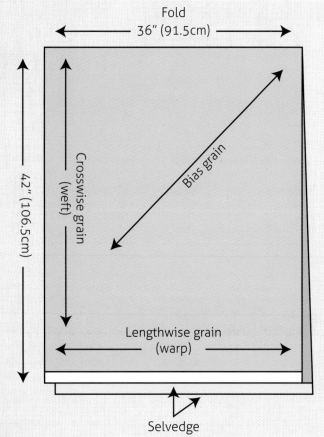

Fold
36" (91.5cm)

42" (106.5cm)

Crosswise grain (weft)

Bias grain

Lengthwise grain (warp)

Selvedge

Fabric anatomy. Try to stay aware of the direction of the grain of your fabric while cutting. This will ensure that your patchwork pieces don't stretch out while you sew.

Truing up: Before your fabric yardage can be cut into precise strips and squares, it will need to be trued. This is the process of making sure your fabric edges are exactly parallel and perpendicular to the selvedges. If you're just starting out, you might want to bone up on your fabric vocabulary and check out how to properly use a rotary cutter (page 34) before embarking on this process.

1. **Fold the fabric.** Fold your fabric in half lengthwise so the selvedge edges meet each other. You might notice that the fabric seems warped when you try to match the selvedges this way. This is very common.

2. **Adjust the selvedges.** Shift the upper selvedge edge to the right or left until the folded edge of the fabric is completely straight and smooth. You might notice that the cut edge of your fabric is now uneven—that's okay, it's what we're expecting. Turn the fabric so the uneven cut edge is on your dominant side. Now place your folded fabric yardage onto the cutting mat so the selvedge lines up exactly with one of the grid lines.

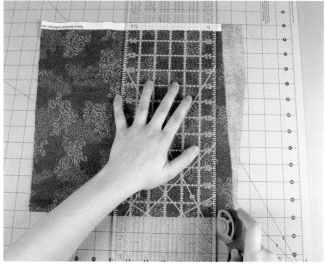

3. **Place the ruler.** Place your quilting ruler on top of the fabric. Position the long edge of the ruler perfectly perpendicular to the selvedge edge of your fabric; make sure the uneven cut edge of the fabric extends beyond the ruler on your dominant side. Use the guidelines on the cutting mat and ruler to make sure both your ruler and fabric are perfectly straight and aligned with one another.

4. **Cut off the edge.** Cut off the uneven fabric edge by running your rotary blade along the ruler, moving away from your body (see Steps 3–5 of the rotary cutting sidebar). The cut edges of your fabric should now be perfectly perpendicular to the selvedge edges. You'll know you have it right when the cut edge of your folded fabric is perfectly straight and there is no kink at the fold. Once you've trued your fabric, any strips and squares cut from it will be exactly on grain.

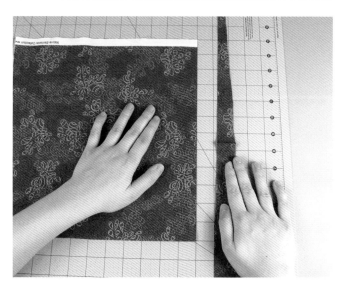

ROTARY CUTTING

Making correct versus incorrect rotary cuts can mean the difference between perfectly straight, precise strips and squares and unfortunate finger cuts and nicked blades. Follow the steps below to use your rotary cutter in the safest and most effective way possible. Remember to use the safety latch and replace the blade as soon as it becomes dull.

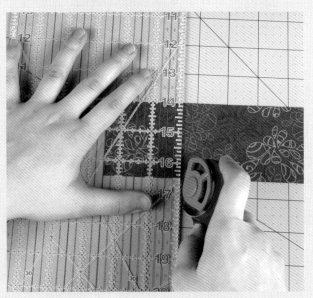

1. **Position your fabric.** Fold your fabric in half lengthwise so the selvedge edges meet each other. Place the trued edge on your non-dominant side with the fold and selvedges parallel to one another. Strips are typically cut from the crosswise grain to be more manageable, although they can also be cut on the lengthwise grain for especially long pieces.

2. **Place the ruler.** Put your quilting ruler on top of the fabric. Align the horizontal measurement guides with the selvedge edge and folded edge of the fabric to achieve the measurement you need for your strip. You can typically cut through four layers of quilting cotton at a time.

3. **Position yourself.** Stand up, place your non-dominant hand on the ruler, and put steady pressure on it to hold it in place. Your fingers should be outstretched, but make sure none of them extend beyond the edge of the ruler.

4. **Cut the fabric.** Using your dominant hand, run the rotary cutter along the side of the ruler, moving it away from your body. Apply light pressure as you move the rotary cutter; the blade is much sharper than you think, and using too much pressure could actually cause you to slice off slivers of your plastic ruler.

5. **Remove the strip.** While still holding the ruler in place, set down the cutter and lightly tug on the fabric to see if it pulls away from the cut strip. If it's still attached, run the cutter over the fabric again using slightly more pressure. If your blade no longer cuts well, even when you're using the right pressure, you'll want to replace it.

6. **Cut any squares.** To cut squares from the strip, turn it 90 degrees. Place your quilting ruler as before and trim off the rough edge of the strip. Then cut squares from the strip in the same way you cut strips from the main fabric.

Quilt Anatomy: What Makes a Quilt?

In the bare bones sense, a quilt is a type of blanket made by layering two pieces of fabric and sewing them together by stitching through both layers across the expanse of the fabric (called quilting). But the common quilts you see, and the ones that have been keeping us warm for generations, are those that comprise a sandwich of fabric, with two outer layers of woven fabric and a layer of batting in between. The quilt top is often made by piecing fabric scraps together. The quilting that joins the three layers is done for added strength and decoration.

A traditional quilt will have some common elements you can easily see from one example to the next, such as sashing, borders, and the like. You can decide to use these elements in your own quilts or go completely modern and throw the rules out the window. Feel free to combine elements to make the quilt of your dreams!

Backing: The piece of cloth used for the back of a quilt.

Batting: The thin, fluffy material placed between the quilt top and the back to provide cushion and possibly warmth to the quilt.

Binding: The strip of fabric that binds the raw edges of the quilt top, batting, and backing.

Border: An outline sewn around the perimeter of a quilt to frame the blocks found inside.

Post: A contrasting block added at the intersection of sashing pieces.

Quilt block: A square of patchwork, often repeated in a grid-like design, that makes up the majority of a quilt composition.

Quilting: The stitching that anchors the three layers of the quilt and holds them together.

Quilt top: The side of the quilt that is meant to be prominently displayed. It may or may not be created from patchwork.

Sashing: A narrow strip added between quilt blocks to make the block stand out or as a way to provide the admirer with a visual resting place between blocks.

Quilt anatomy. These are the typical features you may see in a traditional quilt. Because we're going modern, feel free to use some of these, or none at all, to design your masterpiece!

Fundamental Techniques

Some techniques are a bit harder than others, but each one will build your foundation skills until you're ready to tackle the full quilt projects found in this book. Making a full quilt can be boiled down to three basic steps: piecing, quilting, and binding. This chapter will walk you through eight useful techniques to make these steps easy and achievable—before you know it you'll be ready to tackle a full-size bed quilt! Let's get started with the first step...

Basic Piecing

The most fundamental technique in patchwork is piecing—the process of sewing small bits of fabric together to create larger fabric pieces following a constant cycle of pinning, sewing, and pressing. The resulting pieces can be used in a quilt top, but they're also great for lots of other sewing projects. Patchwork can be done with loads of different shapes: squares, strips, triangles, semicircles, amoebas, you name it. But for beginners, straight seams, especially squares and rectangles, are the way to go. Don't think this will limit you—you'll be amazed by how many fantastic projects you can make using basic shapes! So grab your machine, a bit of fabric, and your thread, and get ready to start! In this section, we will explore:

Simple strip and square piecing: Sewing together rectangular strips and squares.

Foundation piecing: Using a paper foundation as a sewing guide for quick and easy piecing.

Fusible web and freezer paper appliqué: Sewing one fabric shape on top of a background fabric as embellishment.

The ¼" (6mm) seam

Why ¼" (6mm)? In patchwork, ¼" (6mm) seam allowances are standard when piecing fabric bits together. This was decided upon by quilters long ago because it lends just enough fabric to create a strong seam, but not so much that fabric is wasted. Almost every quilt pattern uses a scant ¼" (6mm) seam allowance when accuracy is a factor. It's possible to use a larger seam allowance by adjusting your pattern, as long as you keep it consistent while you sew. There are a number of reasons why you should be precise.

Accuracy for composition: In most quilts you see or make, every block is intended to be the same size and shape to obtain the desired look and composition. To achieve this, every fabric piece you cut must be precise, and every seam allowance you sew with must be a scant ¼" (6mm). With precise cuts and accurate seam allowances, you'll create a quilt where every block is repeated perfectly.

Accuracy for fabric integrity: If your quilt blocks aren't accurate in size, you might end up with wobbly patchwork. As mentioned in the Fabric Anatomy section (page 32), fabric can sometimes stretch while you sew it, especially if your pieces aren't the proper size due to inaccurate cutting or seam allowances. Your finished quilt top won't lie perfectly flat; it will be wavy and bubbly, which is not a fun thing to tame.

All this scanty business: You may be wondering why the ¼" (6mm) seam is often called a "scant" ¼" (6mm) seam. This is because the turning of the fabric and the thickness of the thread use up just a hair's width of fabric. So if you sew a seam slightly smaller than ¼" (6mm) to account for this, your finished patchwork will end up perfect.

Sewing a scant ¼" (6mm) seam may sound daunting, but don't worry! There are loads of easy ways to get that exact scant ¼" (6mm) seam allowance without having to agonize over it.

- **Check your foot:** Your standard presser foot might already be a scant ¼" (6mm) from the needle to the edge. Simply tuck your ruler underneath your machine and measure out a scant ¼" (6mm) from the needle to see where it lands. If the presser foot is wider, try some of the other methods listed below.

- **Masking tape:** Tape a piece of low-adhesive tape (such as painter's tape or artist's tape) along the scant ¼" (6mm) mark.

- **Rubber band:** Wrap a wide rubber band around the free arm of your machine where the scant ¼" (6mm) mark lies.

- **Piecing foot:** If your machine didn't come with this foot, you could buy a compatible piecing foot, also called a ¼" foot. It comes with a ridge on the side that you can run the edge of your fabric against for the perfect seam allowance every time.

Testing your seam allowance: Once you have the tools in place to make a perfect seam allowance, it's time to test it out. To make sure your seam allowance is just right, measure the *finished* product and not the seam allowance itself. For instance, pin and sew together two 2½" (6.4cm) squares with the scant ¼" (6mm) seam. Press the newly sewn seam, and then press the squares open. Measure the two squares lengthwise down the center; you should get 4½" (11.6cm) total. If the measurement is longer, you'll want to adjust your seam allowance guide to create a slightly larger seam. If the measurement is shorter, adjust your guide to create a slightly smaller seam. Continue testing your seam allowance guide until you get it exactly right.

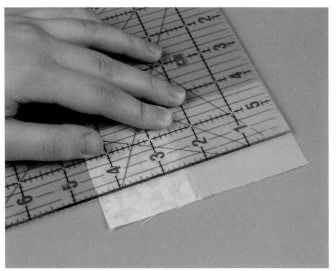

Measure your seam allowance. To be sure you have a correct seam allowance, measure the pieces after they've been sewn together and see if it all adds up right.

Stitch dynamics

All you need to make fantastic patchwork projects for years is a simple straight stitch. This will be the workhorse of your piecing. Most machines will let you adjust the length of your straight stitch, usually by the millimeter, in a range of 0–4mm or 0–5mm. A length of 2–2.5mm is ideal for patchwork. Other machines measure in stitches per inch, which can range from incredibly tiny buttonhole stitches (90 stitches per inch) to long basting stitches (4 stitches per inch). A setting of 10–12 stitches per inch is a perfect middle range.

Pressing seams

After you finish sewing your first patchwork seam, you'll need to take it to your ironing station for the last leg of the pin, sew, and press cycle. Begin by pressing your finished seam right over the stitches with the fabric pieces still closed, with their right sides facing. This will set your seam, allowing the thread to sink into your fabric a little, and get rid of any puckers or warping you might have accidentally run in to. You can use a bit of steam if your iron has this option, but a quick spritz from a water bottle is a cleaner option, as the water doesn't have to travel through the iron's machinery.

The next step for pressing your seam is to open the fabric pieces you have stitched together and press the seam allowances either *open* or *to one side*. This is actually hotly debated in the quilting community, as newer, modern quilters tend to press their seams open, and the traditionalists tend to press to one side. I personally prefer to press my seams open (particularly to reduce bulk), unless the patchwork behaves better with the seams pressed to one side. With certain techniques, like paper foundation piecing (page 40), you must press to one side because of the way the sewing is done. Try out some small projects, pressing the seams both ways, and see what you prefer. If you do decide to press your seams to one side, press them toward the darker fabric of the pieces you have sewn together; this will hide the seam.

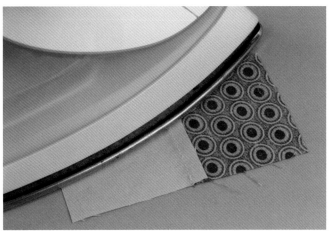

Seams pressed to the side. This is the more traditional method of quilting. Pressing to one side offers strength and "locked seams," but can create bulkiness.

Seams pressed open. This method is often adopted by modern quilters. The seams aren't as strong, but they lie flatter and more predictably.

LOCKING SEAMS

One of the benefits of pressing seams to one side, rather than open, is "locked seams." When you sew one row of squares with the seams allowances pressed to one side and another row with the seam allowances pressed to the other side, the joined rows have seams that then butt together or "lock." To achieve this, you have to plan where to press your seam allowance so each row will lock effectively. Because it takes extra planning, you might see why improvisational modern quilters shy away from it.

PRESSING PROS AND CONS

Pressing Open	Pros	Cons
	Patchwork lies flatter	More time-consuming
	Less bulk	Not as strong
Pressing to One Side	Pros	Cons
	Easier to iron	Extra planning for "locked" seams
	Stronger seams	Extra bulkiness

Chain piecing

Perhaps the most useful trick that quilters may have in their arsenal is chain piecing. The process of pin, sew, press is very repetitive and time consuming, and one way to make it more efficient is doing all the sewing at once without all the thread clipping. Simply set up several pairs of pinned patchwork that are ready to be sewn and follow the process below.

Chain piecing. This simple trick consists of nothing more than tucking your next bit of sewing into your machine right after the previous one. The threads form a chain that can be clipped later.

1. Begin sewing your first pair of patchwork pieces together. Don't forget to remove pins before they reach the presser foot!

2. When you reach the end of the first pair of pieces, leave them under your presser foot and get the next pair.

3. Tuck the new pair under the presser foot, leaving just a bit of space between the new pair and the old pair. Start sewing again, stitching the new pair together. Because you have not clipped the threads between them, the fabric pairs will be joined together in a short "chain." You may want to pull lightly on the first pair as you hold and stitch the second pair.

4. Continue in this manner until all the pairs are sewn together and joined in a chain.

5. When you've finished sewing, clip the threads between each pair to separate them from the chain.

Foundation Piecing

How would you feel if I told you there is a piecing technique so simple it feels like cheating? Using it, you'll be able to sew perfectly accurate seams without worrying about seam allowances, fabric grain, or measuring—and it's all done by sewing on paper! That's the beauty of foundation piecing, a technique more than 100 years old that uses a foundation (either scrap muslin or paper) as a sewing guide while you construct your quilt block. The foundation also acts as a stabilizer, making this technique perfect for off-grain fabric scraps and unconventional fabrics. We'll use paper; don't confuse this technique with English paper piecing or the foundation piecing done using muslin instead of paper.

A paper foundation pieced block starts with a pattern either traced or printed on a paper foundation—the block is typically constructed outward from a single (usually central) point. More and more fabric pieces are added by sewing along the pattern lines until the entire sheet of paper is covered. With foundation piecing, you manage to sew sharp angles and tiny shapes with complete ease!

The paper

One disadvantage of foundation piecing is that it uses a lot of paper. There are many paper options to choose from, depending on your budget and preference. Thin papers tend to work better than thick papers, as the thin stuff is easier to rip away from the fabric once the block is finished.

Newspaper: The quilters of yesteryear used newspaper for their foundation piecing. With a good light box or window, you can trace your foundation pattern onto the paper and start sewing from there. Newspaper rips easily and sews well, but it cannot be run through your printer without risk of jamming and tearing.

Tracing paper: This is similar to newspaper in thickness, but is much easier to see through, making placing the fabric very easy during sewing. It does not work well with printers, though.

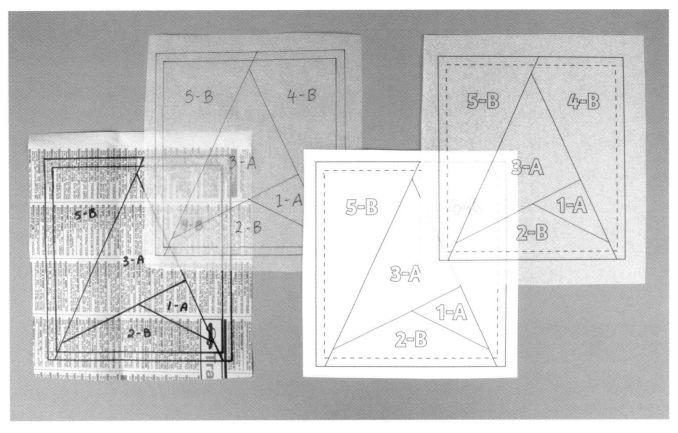

Foundation piecing papers. Select what paper to use for your foundation piecing based on what works best for your skill and budget. From left to right: newspaper, tracing paper, printer paper, foundation piecing paper.

Printer paper: While not as easy to tear away as newspaper or tracing paper, printer paper is obviously easy to print on and cheap, if not free, because you can use the back of any scrap paper lying around the house: memos, letters, flyers, notices, or anything else you have on hand. For best results, use the thinnest paper you can find with as little ink on it as possible so it's easy to see through.

Foundation piecing paper: Quilt shops often sell a kind of paper specifically made for foundation piecing. It's much like tracing paper, but runs through your printer easily so making multiple copies is a cinch. The downside? You can't get it free the way you can scrap paper!

The pattern

Finding a pattern: You can find foundation piecing patterns in books like this or online. Foundation piecing patterns show outlines of each segment with numbers that show the sewing order—just like a paint-by-number template.

Preparing your pattern: When you've found a pattern, you can trace it onto your chosen piecing paper using a light box or sunny window, or print it onto the paper using your home printer/copier. Digital patterns are easiest to work with because you can print them directly on your home printer—print as many copies as the project stipulates. Before you start sewing, trim your pattern generally around the cutting line, about ¼" (0.5cm) outside the line or so. If you're using opaque paper, consider tracing the pattern lines onto both sides.

The patchwork

1 **Cover the first section.** With the wrong side of the paper facing up, decide what fabric you want to sew on section 1. Cut a scrap of fabric at least ½" (1.5cm) larger than that section on all sides (bigger is better as a beginner). Pin it (or use basting glue) face up onto the paper pattern.

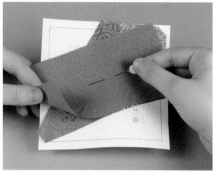

2 **Layer the second fabric.** Look for where section 1 joins section 2; we're going to be sewing on that line. Cut a scrap of fabric for section 2 as you did for section 1. Pin it onto the fabric from section 1 (right sides together), lining up the raw edges so that they cover that sewing line.

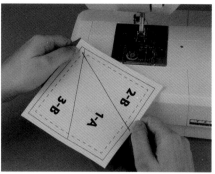

3 **Sew along the guideline.** Turn the paper over, and sew along the printed guideline between sections 1 and 2 using a short stitch, about 1–1.5mm or 25–15 stitches per inch. This perforates the paper, making it easier to rip off later. Start about ¼" (0.5cm) before the sewing line and stop ¼" (0.5cm) after for insurance.

4 **Trim the seam allowance.** Fold back the section 2 area along the stitching line and use your quilting ruler to trim the seam allowance down to ¼" (6mm).

5 **Press the seam.** Open out the fabric pieces and press them as you usually would. If you look at your traced lines, you'll see that your second fabric now covers all of section 2.

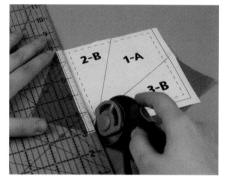

6 **Trim the block.** Repeat Steps 2–5 for the remaining sections of the pattern. Finally, with the paper facing up, trim off the excess fabric along the cutting line.

7 **Complete the block.** To finish, carefully rip the paper off the back of the block. Your quilt block is now complete! You can sew it just like any other quilt block now; here, four of the blocks were sewn to create this star pattern.

Fusible Web Appliqué

Another quilting technique that will unlock loads more project possibilities for you is appliqué. It's the process of sewing one fabric shape on top of a background fabric as embellishment, and it's the perfect way to add curvy or detailed shapes that would otherwise be difficult to sew in patchwork.

The quilting world has dozens of ways to handle appliqué, but this book will cover two of the most flexible methods: using fusible web or freezer paper (page 45). Fusible web appliqué is perfect for sewing especially tiny shapes that have sharp details.

Supplies

For beautiful appliqué you only need a few supplies to get started. You shouldn't have any trouble finding these at your local fabric store or quilting shop.

Fabric: The same fabrics used for quilting can also be used for appliqué, though choosing a fabric that's as thin as, or slightly thinner than, your background fabric will make the job easier, as it will reduce bulk while you sew. Quilting cotton, flannel, thin corduroy, and batiste are all excellent choices. Felt is a great choice too, and has the added benefit of not fraying along its raw edges. This is ideal for beginners because it requires little to no sewing.

Fusible web: Fusible web is a kind of paper-backed adhesive, that, when adhered to your appliqué fabric, turns the fabric into an iron-on patch of sorts. Heavy-duty fusible web will hold your fabric in place indefinitely, with no sewing necessary. This works best for projects that won't get a lot of wear and tear. Light fusible web will hold your fabric in place temporarily so it doesn't shift or pucker while you sew it to your background fabric, making it ideal for quilts. You can find fusible web in precut sheets or by the yard.

Fusible web applique. Light fabrics such as cotton, flannel, and thin corduroy are best for fusible web appliqué—especially paired with lightweight fusible web. Felt is best paired with heavy-duty fusible web for embellishments on projects that won't get a lot of washing.

Prepping

Putting fusible web to use is pretty easy once you understand how it works. Gather up your appliqué pattern; even a hand-drawn doodle or outline will do. Note that this method will create a reverse image of your appliqué pattern, so be sure to flip images that are asymmetrical, text in particular.

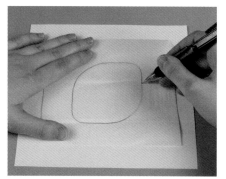

1 **Trace the pattern.** Your fusible web sheet will have a rough side (the adhesive side) and a smooth one (the paper side). Trace your appliqué pattern on the smooth paper side.

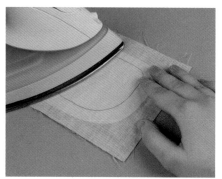

2 **Iron the fusible web.** Cut generally around the traced shape, then place the fusible web over your appliqué fabric with the adhesive side facing the wrong side of the fabric. Iron according to the package directions, usually by letting a medium-hot iron rest in place for a few seconds.

3 **Iron the appliqué.** Cut along the traced lines of your pattern. Peel off the paper, leaving the adhesive behind. Iron the embellishment with the adhesive facing the right side of your project fabric. If you've used heavy-duty fusible web, you can leave your project as is. If you've used lightweight fusible web, you'll need to sew the edge of the appliqué to reinforce it.

Sewing

Straight stitch: Using a regular presser foot, sew around the outline of your appliqué piece using a straight stitch about 1⁄16"–1⁄8" (2–3mm) away from the raw edge. This takes some careful coordination, so don't be afraid to stop and rotate your work when necessary. This method will leave your appliqué with exposed raw edges, so unless you want that look (see the Clamshell Rug, page 74, for an example), use felt, which won't fray.

Straight stitch. A straight stitch around your appliqué piece is a simple and fast technique, but might leave some ragged edges on quilting cotton.

Zigzag stitch: You can also sew around your appliqué with a medium-width zigzag stitch that's 1–1.5mm long. This will encase the raw edges of your fabric in thread so it's less likely to fray over time. Align the zigzag so the outside edge of the stitch is just outside the appliqué edge—this should completely cover the raw edge. Be sure to stop and pivot at corners with the needle down, so the stitches look neater.

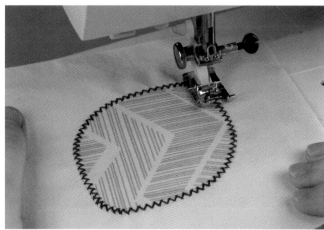

Zigzag stitch. A zigzag stitch takes a bit longer, but will cover the raw edges of your appliqué fabric, preventing any fraying.

Freezer Paper Appliqué

If fusible web appliqué wasn't quite up your alley, you'll be happy to know there's another form of appliqué that's also beginner friendly. Freezer paper appliqué not only avoids having to buy sheets and sheets of fusible web, it also looks much cleaner because all the raw edges are neatly tucked under the shape. Hand-turned appliqué is the hand-sewn version of this method, but the version I describe here is made fast and easy for machine sewers!

This type of appliqué works best for shapes without sharp curves or corners. Smooth, round curves are the ideal way to go. This method also lends itself well to large appliqué shapes, because it's reusable and more economical than fusible web.

Supplies

Fabric: Much like with fusible web appliqué, a fabric that's as thin as or thinner than your background fabric is best. However, because the fabric edges will be turned under, try to steer clear of anything too thick that won't fold easily. Quilting cotton, chambray, voile, and poplin are ideal.

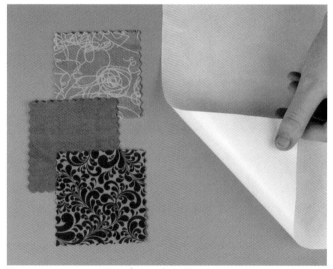

Freezer paper appliqué supplies. Freezer paper appliqué only requires appliqué fabric (quilting cotton or other thin fabrics are best) and freezer paper.

Freezer paper: Freezer paper is actually an amazing little product. It was originally used before plastic wrap and other food storage technology took off, but on fabric it does wonderful things. The waxy side of the paper, when ironed, temporarily adheres weakly to fabric. It's perfect for making templates or marking patterns, and then it can be easily peeled away; it's like a sticky note for fabric! Freezer paper can be found in dedicated quilt shops as well as in grocery stores.

Prepping

There are many ways freezer paper can help you with your patchwork, but to get perfectly turned appliqué here's what you'll need to do:

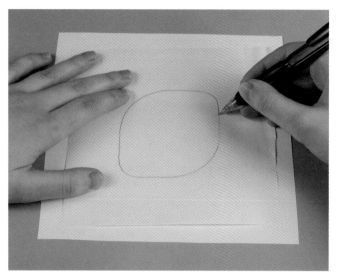

1 **Trace the pattern.** The sheet of freezer paper will have a waxy side (the shiny one) and a paper side (which is matte). Trace your appliqué pattern on the paper side.

2 **Iron the freezer paper.** Cut out the traced shape, then iron it with the waxy side facing down onto the wrong side of your appliqué fabric. Let the iron, set at medium to high heat, rest on top of the freezer paper for a few seconds without steam to adhere it in place. The paper shouldn't fall off when you finish.

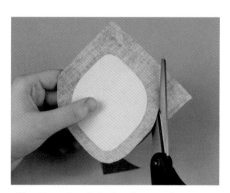

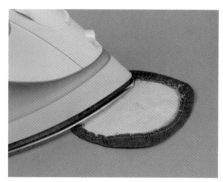

3 **Cut the fabric shape.** Cut around the appliqué pattern, giving yourself a ½" (1.5cm) seam allowance or so (you can cut smaller as you gain experience).

4 **Gather the seam allowance.** Run a basting stitch—either by hand or by machine—around the perimeter of the seam allowance you've given yourself. When you make it all the way around, tighten the thread so the fabric bunches up and around the paper pattern.

5 **Press the gathers.** The gathering will help create smooth curves around the rounded portions of your pattern; use the iron to press those in place until they're perfectly flat. When finished, remove the paper carefully without ruining the folds. You're now ready to sew!

Sewing

Once the turning is done, how you sew your appliqué is open to your imagination! You don't have to worry about frayed edges, so any stitch you like will work. Here are a few stitch suggestions. Be sure to pin or glue baste the appliqué in place where you need it so you know it's smoothly held in place.

Straight stitch: Using a regular presser foot, sew around the outline of your appliqué piece using a straight stitch about ¹⁄₁₆"–¹⁄₈" (2–3mm) away from the folded edge. This takes some careful coordination, so don't be afraid to stop and rotate your work when necessary.

Hem stitch: This stitch is usually used in sewing machines to perform a blind hem, but for appliqué, it's the one machine stitch that looks the least noticeable (especially if you use the right thread). The machine will stitch straight for a few stitches, and then go sideways to make one zigzag. Align the needle so it sews just outside the outer edge of the appliqué piece and takes the zigzag stitch onto the appliqué fabric.

Slip stitch: This hand-sewn method results in a nearly invisible seam. The stitch is done by taking a small ¹⁄₁₆"–¹⁄₈" (2–3mm) stitch into the fold of the appliqué fabric, then going across and taking another stitch from the background fabric. Repeat this process as you go around the appliqué shape, gently tugging the thread to tighten it. The threads should sink right into the fabric, nearly invisible!

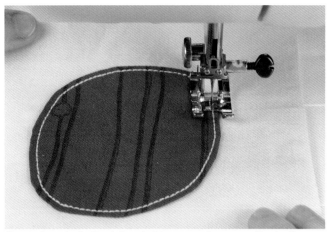

Straight stitch. Straight stitching around your appliqué offers a clean and simple look.

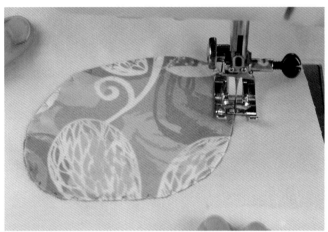

Hem stitch. A hem stitch is a slightly less visible machine stitch for your appliqué.

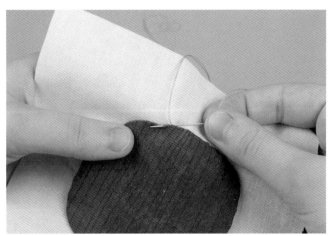

Slip stitch. A hand-sewn slip stitch is the ultimate way to make sure the stitching on your appliqué looks invisible.

Quilting

After finishing your patchwork, the next major step in creating a quilt is called quilting. This is the process of layering your patchwork with some kind of backing material and typically a layer of batting in between, and then stitching through all those layers to hold them in place. This process not only holds all the layers of the quilt together, making it smoother, it also strengthens the quilt immensely, making it less likely to fray and fall apart over time. Once the layers are basted, they can then be quilted in lots of different ways.

Piecing the quilt back: If you can't find material large enough to fit your project as the backing, you'll need to piece your quilt back from cotton yardage. Get some tips below.

Quilt tying: Instead of stitching through the layers of your quilt, finish it more quickly using single knots tied through the layers.

Machine quilting: Stitching through the layers of your quilt with a sewing machine to create patterns of stitches over the entire piece.

Quilt-as- you-go: A non-traditional technique used to make quilting more manageable.

Planning Your Quilt Back

As you begin to consider making your first quilt, keep in mind that when the top is finished you'll need a quilt back as well. As stated at the beginning of the chapter, special extra-wide quilt backing material is available for large quilts. Quantities for extra-wide fabrics are given for the quilt projects in this book, but the limited colors offered might not work for what you had planned. If you want more options, you'll need to piece the quilt back from whatever fabric yardage you have.

Piecing

1. **Determine the quilt back size.** Measure your quilt top, then plan for a quilt back that's roughly 10" (25cm) larger both horizontally and vertically to account for any shifting that the quilt top might do as you sew (Figure A). (The larger your quilt top, the more important is it so have at least 10 inches [25cm] of play.) For this example, we will calculate for a 57" x 76" (145 x 193cm) quilt top; it requires a 67" x 86" (170 x 218cm) piece of fabric for the quilt back.

2. **Find your preferred quilt back material.** Decide what material you'd like to use for the quilt back. Quilting cotton is best here, as you'll want something sturdy. Measure the width of this fabric and subtract 2" (5cm) from this number to account for seam allowances. For quilting cotton that's 40" (101.5cm) wide (after trimming the selvedges and pre-shrinking), this becomes 38" (96.5cm).

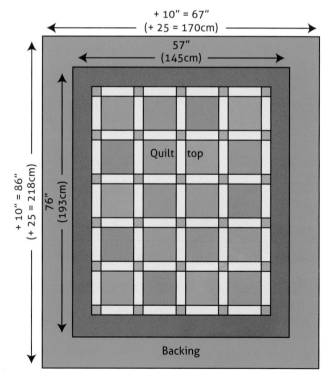

Figure A.

3. **Divide your quilt width/length by this number.**
   Divide the width and length of your quilt back by the measurement derived in the previous step and determine which one has the smallest remainder. In our example, the calculations are as follows: 67 divided by 38 equals 1.76, and 86 divided by 38 equals 2.26. The side with the smallest remainder will be the direction where we spread the lengthwise grain of the backing fabric. Once calculated, round your answer down to the nearest whole number. For our example, to sew panels across the length of our sample quilt we would need 1.76 pieces, but across the width would require 2.26 pieces. We'll sew two panels across the width of the quilt and deal with the small gap in Step 5 (see Figure B). Your quilt back might not even have a gap—lucky! If that's the case, go ahead and skip to Step 6.

4. **Determine the yardage.** Multiply the measurement of the quilt going across the lengthwise grain by the rounded-down number calculated in Step 3. Divide this number by 36 for inches (100 for metric) to determine the amount you'll need for the majority of the quilt back. For our example, with two panels across the width of our sample quilt, you would calculate as follows for inches: 67" x 2 = 134"; 134" divided by 36 equals 3.75 or 3¾, so you will need 3¾ yd. For the metric system, 170cm x 2 = 340cm; 340cm divided by 100 equals 3.4, so you will need 3.4m.

5. **Plan for the gaps.** To fill in the leftover gap, this is where the magic of improvisational modern quilting comes in. Simply use scraps of fabric from the quilt top to make an interesting band of color for the back. Subtract the width of the main yardage from the quilt back requirement, add an extra 2" (5cm) or so for insurance, and plan to make a strip of patchwork by that width; perhaps try out some new quilt blocks or just go with simple strips (Figure C).

6. **Assemble the back.** Sew the large panels and contrast strip together with a ½" (1.3cm) seam allowance for added strength. Press the seams, and then use it for your quilt assembly.

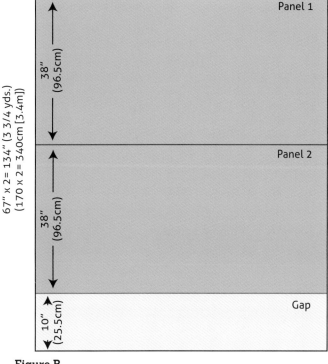

Figure B.

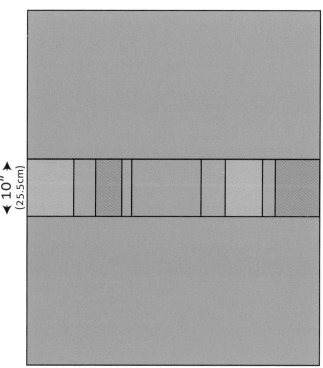

Figure C.

Making the Quilt Sandwich

The fundamental part of starting the quilting of your project, whether it ends up tied or machine quilted, is making the quilt sandwich. The tips here are ideal for handling especially large quilts so all the layers line up perfectly. Giving it your all during this step will ensure that the rest of your quilting goes smoothly.

1 Fold the layers. Cut your backing fabric 10" (25cm) larger and your batting 8" (20.5cm) larger than your quilt top. Fold all sections into quarters to find the center lines. Note that the backing is folded with the right side facing out and the quilt top is folded with the wrong side facing out.

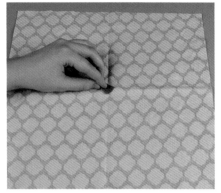

2 Lay out the backing fabric. Place your quilt backing fabric right side down on the biggest flat surface you have, such as a dining room table for smaller projects or a hardwood floor for bigger projects. Mark the center point with a pin or bit of masking tape.

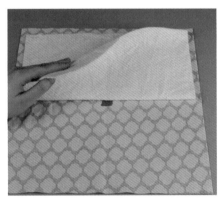

3 Lay out the batting. Place the corner fold of your batting at the point you've marked in the middle of the backing. Using the center creases as guides, unfold the batting over the surface of the backing fabric. Remove the center marking from the backing and move it to the batting center.

4 Tape the layers. Smooth out the batting and backing layers as much as possible; the edges don't have to align perfectly, but be sure to feel for any bumps or wrinkles. When finished, tape the edges of the batting and backing with painter's tape so the layers are taut.

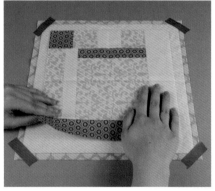

5 Lay out the quilt top. Place the corner fold of your quilt top at the point you've marked in the middle of the batting. Using the center creases as guides, unfold the quilt top over the batting. When finished, smooth out the patchwork as best you can. There should be several inches of batting and backing extending beyond the patchwork.

Quilt Tying

Quilting your first project can be a little daunting, because you're basically layering three sheets together and trying to keep everything smooth while sewing them together all at the same time. Quilt tying takes away a bit of the stress by eliminating the need for quilting through rows of stitching—instead the stitches are replaced by single knots dotted throughout your quilt.

Supplies

To sandwich your quilt for the first time, not only will you need your finished patchwork (the quilt top), but also the batting and backing fabric. Quilt tying is quite good at taming especially fluffy quilt batting, so feel free to break out this technique when you've got high-loft polyester.

Needle: In order to thread the string through your quilt, you'll need to find a long, strong needle with a big eye. Tapestry needles work fine, but in the quilting section of your store you'll find special needles designed specifically for hand-tying.

String: A quilt can successfully be tied with different kinds of strong material. Embroidery floss and pearl cotton (you may see it spelled *perle*, too) offer color selection, but aren't very colorfast. Thin yarns offer texture, but may not hold up well over time. Crochet cotton is considered the best choice. The fun part is looking through all the specialty yarns that can add a bit of pop to your project! No matter what you choose, make sure it will fit through the eye of your tapestry needle.

1 Mark the tie points. Mark points on your quilt about 5" (12.5cm) apart in any configuration you like, such as a grid, a brick pattern, or centered in key points on your patchwork. (Instead of a ruler, you can also simply use your fist as a guide.) Either way, mark the points with large Xs using a fabric marker.

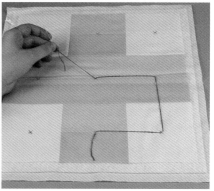

2 Thread the needle. Thread your needle with the string; leave one end long and fold the end at the needle's eye over about 3" (7.5cm). Working from the front of the quilt top, make a stitch at your first marked point, and leave a long thread tail. Continue jumping from X to X, making one stitch at a time until all the Xs are stitched.

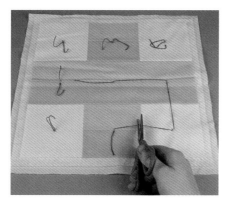

3 Cut the strands. Cut each length of string visible on top of the patchwork halfway along its length, making sure to leave the tails in place.

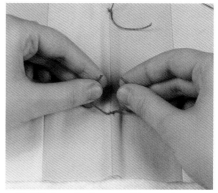

4 Make the knots. Tie each pair of tails into a sturdy square knot.

Machine Quilting

Ratcheting up the complexity, machine quilting is a step up from quilt tying. While it takes a bit of practice to get used to working on a large canvas like a quilt, this technique has many possibilities

Prepping

See page 50 for info about making your quilt sandwich. After accomplishing that, instead of quilt tying, you'll baste the layers so the quilt can be taken to your sewing machine later.

When machine quilting, you need to have some way to temporarily hold the quilt layers together so everything stays flat and smooth when you take it to your machine. It's just like using pins with regular seams, but you need something a bit stronger and safer.

Safety pins: These are the go-to tool for most quilt basting. Regular safety pins will work just fine, but special curved safety pins for quilters are commonly seen in stores. They are available in a few sizes; select the one best suited to the thickness of your quilt. Simply pin through all the layers of your quilt about every 5"–7" (12.5–18cm) for even coverage.

Basting spray: Not all quilters like to use spray basting, especially for bigger quilts, but for small quilts it makes the basting process quite easy. Mist the spray onto both sides of your quilt batting, then press it into your quilt top and backing as described in the quilt sandwiching steps on page 50.

Straight-line machine quilting

The easiest way to break into machine quilting is to stick to straight lines. With some easy guides and a little bit of practice, you'll be working through your quilt in no time!

1. **Set up your guidelines.** Do yourself a favor and set up distinct guidelines beforehand so there's no question of where you need to sew when you start quilting. Ask yourself how much quilting you want and how many guidelines to use. Refer to your batting product information, which will usually give a maximum quilting distance before the batting runs the risk of bunching or bearding during washing. If you prefer puffier, comforter-like quilts, lean toward the high end of this maximum distance. Quilts with dense quilting (½" [1.5cm] apart or less) will last longer but will take much longer to finish. This will also shrink bed-sized quilts by a noticeable amount; around 1"–2" (2.5–5cm) depending on the density of the quilting. Here are two types of guidelines.

•   **Seam lines as guides.** Quilting right on the seams you've sewn for your quilt top is known as *stitching in the ditch.* While it's a common technique, bulky seams can work against you and often throw you off track. It's much better to try *outline quilting,* where you stitch just outside the seams (using the presser foot as a guide).

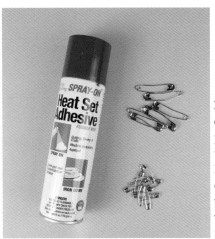

Basting tools. You can use either safety pins or basting spray to baste your quilt layers. Which to choose will depend on your preference, as well as the size and thickness of your quilt.

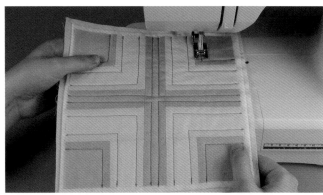

Outline quilting. This is done by quilting right alongside your seam lines using the presser foot as a guide. It's practically foolproof and looks fantastic.

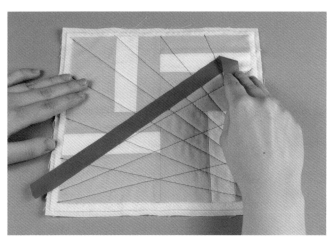

Masking tape guides. For other straight lines, such as a diamond pattern, consider using masking tape to serve as guidelines that can be removed later.

- **Masking tape.** Straight lines that go across your quilt make a huge graphic impact that looks beautiful on modern-style quilts. Try using masking tape or painter's tape to run perfectly straight lines down your quilt.

2. **Install a walking foot.** As mentioned in the getting started section (page 18), a walking foot is a special presser foot that ensures an even feed of your quilting layers, preventing puckers and warping from the top layer down to the bottom. When doing straight line quilting, the consistency you get with this foot will really come in handy.

3. **Start sewing.** With your quilt all basted, marked, and ready to quilt, it's time to get it under your machine and get started. Use a slightly longer than average stitch (about 3mm or 9 stitches per inch) and a needle of a slightly larger size (80/12–90/14) to get through all those layers. You can use a strong neutral thread so the stitches blend into your quilt, or a contrasting thread if you want to show off your work. Now, here are some things to keep in mind.

Quilting plan. When quilting, it's always best to start in the middle and work your way toward the outside to push out any extra fabric and prevent puckers. As the numbers here indicate, start in the center and work out to the right. Then return to the center and work out to the left.

- **Start from the middle.** While it's a little awkward, in order to prevent puckers and bunching it's better to start from the middle of the quilt and work your way out. In straight line quilting, that means you can start in the middle top of the quilt. If you encounter extra fabric while you sew, push it out to the edges of the quilt instead of letting it cause a pucker.

- **Let the puckers happen.** If you do encounter a pucker in your quilting and it can't be pushed to the side, instead of constantly pushing it downward and letting the problem snowball, it's best to just get it out of the way and sew over that little spot. It's better to have one little pucker and go on with smooth quilting than to have one large pucker and also warp your fabric.

- **Use previous quilt lines as guides.** Utilize every guideline you can while quilting, whether it be the side of your presser foot, the seam from your patchwork, or a previous quilting line. This will ensure that your lines look crisp and straight if you're going for a geometric look.

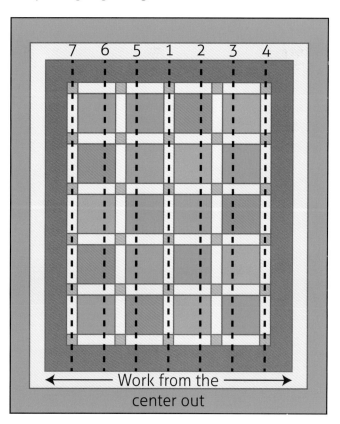

Free-motion machine quilting

While usually considered a slightly more advanced form of quilting, free-motion quilting actually suits some beginners very well. Some people think it feels much more natural than other forms of quilting. It just depends on what kind of sewing personality you have—so give it a try if you feel adventurous. It might be the technique you were waiting for!

1. **Set up your machine.** Make sure everything is set up right on your sewing machine, and set it back when you're done.

   • **Install your darning foot.** This special kind of foot is meant for machine embroidery but also works for free-motion quilting. A little spring ensures it doesn't press on the fabric much at all, giving you exactly the right kind of pressure you need to free-motion quilt.

   • **Lower your feed dogs.** If your machine has this feature, you'll need it so it no longer moves the fabric for you, leaving you to take control. Most machines control the feed dogs through some kind of lever near the bobbin housing. You'll know you have it right when you see the feed dogs resting visibly lower than before.

2. **Find your comfort zone.** This is one of those techniques where you're just going to have to try it out first before you can hope to get the hang of it. Take a test quilt sandwich to the machine and try sewing on it, making little circles or meandering lines. The speed at which you move the quilt determines the stitch length, and the pressure you put on the foot pedal determines the speed of the needle. It's natural to want to go slower on the foot pedal when you're nervous, but you actually want to keep a rather consistent medium-high speed so your stitches aren't too long.

3. **Make a plan.** When you feel ready to start on your actual quilt, get an idea of how you want your quilting to look by researching some samples.

   • **Freehand quilting.** If you have a good rhythm you can try just doodling stitches freehand. *Stippling* is the term used to describe meandering stitches that don't cross each other, and it's the easiest way for beginners to start. Then you can move on to other styles such as geometric stippling or fancier motifs.

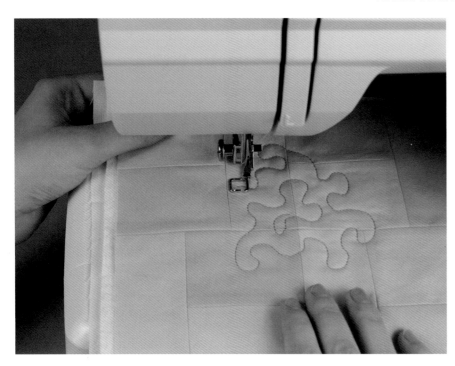

Stippling. The most basic form of freehand quilting, stippling is the process of quilting meandering lines that don't cross. As your skill progresses, consider tweaking this idea in different ways.

- **Quilting by pattern.** You'll see that free-motion quilting patterns run the gamut of simple straight lines to ornate filigree. These are definitely for when you feel more confident in your skills, but you can try designing your own quilting pattern by sketching on your quilt with a fabric pen or chalk, then stitching over the lines.

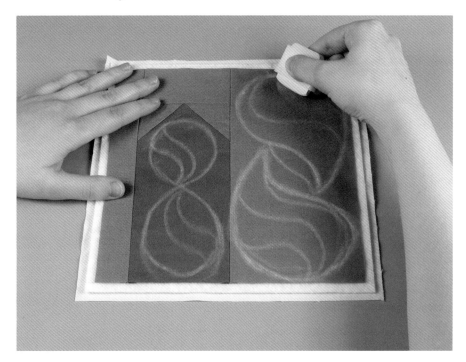

Quilting by pattern. Getting precise quilting stitches by following a pattern is a great goal to strive for as your skills progress. The projects in this book stick with the easier straight-line and freehand quilting, but you can try drawing outlines of your own designs to practice.

LONGARM QUILTING

You may have heard the term longarm quilting. A longarm machine is a very large sewing machine that works the opposite way a regular home sewing machine does: You move the sewing needle that's installed on a long arm across your stationary quilt rather than moving the quilt around underneath a stationary needle. Many say that this form of quilting feels more natural than working on a standard machine because it simulates drawing on paper. You can often rent out time to spend at a longarm machine at your local quilt shop, or they might have options for doing the quilting for you. They'll have certain specifications you'll need to follow, such as the size of your quilt batting and backing, so be sure to do a little research before you prepare those layers.

Quilt-As-You-Go Quilting

The quilt-as-you-go method is a non-traditional technique used to make quilting a whole patchwork project more manageable. There are a few ways to achieve it, but any approach that involves quilting sections of the quilt first and then adding more sections later can be considered a quilt-as-you-go method. This version is one I use the most myself to make creating extra-large quilts much less of a headache.

Prepping

Gather up your choice of batting for the project you're working on. For this kind of quilting, thin batting is best, particularly cotton, or even just flannel yardage.

Sewing

Once you understand how this version of quilt-as-you-go is handled, you'll see it's quite a lot like paper foundation piecing because each part of the quilt works outward from the first piece, slowly getting bigger and bigger. For instance in this example, imagine making a table runner from a row of quilt blocks using the quilt-as-you-go method.

When the strip is complete, you can simply trim away the excess batting and backing and bind it as you usually would, following the technique on page 58. You can also use this process on rows or columns of quilt blocks, working across or down a quilt to build it as you go.

1 **Layer the first block.** After you finish your quilt block (shown in purple), cut a piece of batting and backing fabric (shown in red) that's slightly larger. (You can use a second quilt block as the back instead.) Sandwich the batting with the quilt block and backing facing outward. Align all layers against the edge to the right. Quilt the three layers at this time.

2 **Layer the second block.** Working with a second set of pieces (consisting of another quilt block, batting square, and backing square), layer in this order: the new batting; the new backing, right side up (shown in blue); then the block quilted in the previous step, right side up (in purple/red); and finally the new quilt block, right side down (shown in green). Align all layers against the edge to the right.

3 **Sew the blocks.** Sew along the aligned side of the quilt block through all the layers. Trim away the excess batting if possible to reduce bulk. The seams will still be a little bulky, but on the bright side, the previous block is already quilted and you can simply focus on the block at hand.

4 **Press the layers.** Press the second quilt block fabric away from the first, pressing the seam so everything is nice and flat. Quilt this new block, then repeat Steps 2–4 as many times as you like to get a continuous strip.

Utilizing quilt-as-you-go

If you enjoyed doing the quilt-as-you-go method, you'll see how it can make creating extra-large quilts so much easier! The system I use for larger quilts when I don't have a lot of time or space goes like this; it's fast and also barely takes up any room under the machine's throat space.

1. Plan out your quilt in columns that are about 8"–20" (20–50cm) wide, whether that be by quilt block or a general section of your quilt. Cut your batting and backing accordingly.

2. Layer the first column of the quilt as you would for a whole quilt and quilt it with simple vertical machine quilting, such as straight lines or waves.

3. Using the quilt-as-you-go method, layer and quilt the next column of the quilt, then press the finished section. Run quilting stitches through the next section as you did for the first one.

4. Repeat Step 3 until all the columns of the quilt are complete, and then bind (see page 58) to finish.

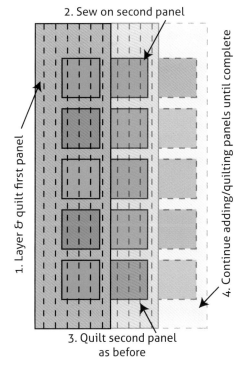

2. Sew on second panel

1. Layer & quilt first panel

3. Quilt second panel as before

4. Continue adding/quilting panels until complete

Large quilt-as-you-go-projects. By quilting only the right-most panel, one at a time, you'll never end up with more quilt under your machine than you can handle.

Binding

After the layers of your quilt are all quilted, you can finally move on to the last step—binding! The most straightforward method of cleaning up those raw edges is to wrap them in a strip of fabric, not only to add extra strength but as a design opportunity as well. You can choose a matching color of fabric so the edge of the quilt looks seamless, or use a contrasting fabric to make the border pop nicely.

Binding anatomy

The strongest and easiest binding to work with is called *double fold binding* or *French fold binding*. This is made from a strip of fabric folded in half lengthwise (with wrong sides together) so one side of the strip has raw edges and the other side has a fold.

Binding that's cut along the crosswise grain (width) of your fabric is generally considered the best choice, because when it does eventually wear out and start to fray, the threads will deteriorate in a centralized location that's easy to repair rather than in a run that goes down your quilt.

The binding is attached by sewing both raw edges to the edge of the quilt, then wrapping it around the edge of the quilt and sewing the folded edge in place on the other side of the quilt.

Calculating how much material you need

A ⅜" (1cm)-wide finished binding is a good happy medium—and it's what I've used for all the projects in this book—though you'll find a lot of seasoned quilters go with a ¼" (6mm) binding.

1. Take the width of the binding you want to make and multiply that by three to account for the three times the binding will cover the quilt edge. So for a ⅜" (1cm) binding: ⅜" x 3 = 1⅛" (1cm x 3 = 3cm).

2. Add ¼" (6mm) to account for the extra fabric needed to wrap the binding (1⅛" + ¼" = 1⅜" [3cm + 0.6cm = 3.6cm]).

3. Then multiply the sum by 2 to account for the double fold (1⅜" x 2 = 2¾") [3.6cm x 2 = 7.2cm]. This will be the width of the strip you'll need for your binding.

Here's the formula to use to find out how much quilting cotton you'll need for your binding:

1. Calculate the perimeter of your quilt (length + width x 2 = ___)

2. Add an extra 15" (38cm) for working room (X + 15"= ___ [X + 38cm = ___])

3. Divide that figure by 40" (101.5cm) as follows (X/40 = ___ [X/101.5 = ___])

4. Round up the answer to the nearest whole number.

5. Multiply that answer by your binding width. In this example, the binding width is 2¾ (7.2cm) like this (X x 2¾" = ___ [X x 7.2cm = ___])

6. Divide the answer by 36" (100cm) to get the number of yards (meters) this way (X/36 = ___ [X/100cm = ___])

7. Round up that figure to the nearest yardage cut—¼, ⅓, ½, ⅔, or ¾ yd. (for metric, round up to the next tenth of a meter)—to give yourself a bit of insurance.

Sewing

This is the basic and reliable method of mitered binding that most quilters use. Start by cutting the strips from your binding fabric in the width you calculated on page 59.

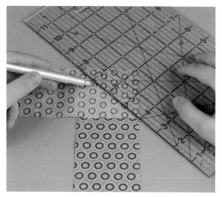

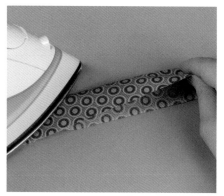

1 **Chain your strips**. To chain a long strip of binding, align the short ends of two pieces together at a right angle. Then, on the top piece, draw a diagonal line going from outside corner to outside corner. This will be your seam line. The inside corner is never used in a diagonal seam. Sew all your strips together, one after the next, this way.

2 **Fold the strip**. After pressing the diagonal seam allowances open, fold the entire strip in half lengthwise with wrong sides together. Iron the entire strip flat to be ready to sew.

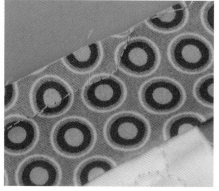

3 **Begin the binding**. Start attaching your binding along the middle of one side of your quilt as follows. Align the edge of the binding along the right side of the quilt and, leaving about 6" (15cm) of the end of your binding unattached, sew using a seam allowance equal to the (finished) binding width. Before you approach the corner, refer to the next step!

4 **Sew the corner**. When you are ⅜" (1cm) away (or a distance equal to your binding width) from the next edge, stop sewing, pivot the quilt, and sew off the edge at a diagonal toward the corner of the quilt.

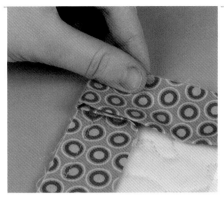

5 **Fold the corner.** To create the mitered edge corner, fold your binding to the side and away from the quilt against the diagonally stitched line. Then fold it back down over itself, aligning the long edge with the next side of the quilt, creating a little triangle fold in the corner.

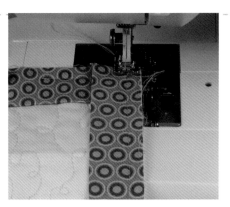

6 **Finish the corner.** To complete the corner, begin stitching the next side of the quilt, sewing over the folds of the miter with plenty of backstitches so the corner is very strong. Then continue stitching the remainder of the binding to the edges of the quilt, mitering at each corner. As you approach your starting point, refer to the next step.

7 **Overlap the ends.** Stop sewing about 12" (30.5cm) short of your starting point. Overlap the starting and finishing ends of your binding on the edge of your quilt. Trim off a bit of extra binding, unfold it, and place it above the overlap (this scrap will serve as a guide). On both sides of the scrap, trim any excess binding that extends beyond its width.

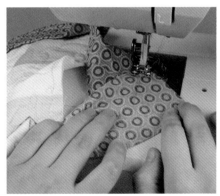

8 **Join the ends.** Unfold and bring together the starting and finishing ends of the binding with right sides facing. Sew them on the diagonal just as in Step 1. Trim the seam allowance, press the seam open, and fold the binding back up lengthwise. Align the unattached binding with the corresponding edge of the quilt and stitch it in place. The binding is now attached completely around the front of the quilt.

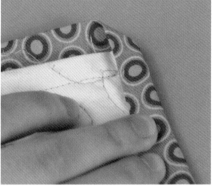

9 **Wrap the binding.** Press the binding away from the quilt, then wrap it around the edge to the back. For the corners, you'll need to fold one side at a time, overlapping the folds as if you were wrapping a package. The folded edge should extend a little beyond the previous seam. Pin and iron the folded binding in place.

10 **Attach the binding.** While traditionalists sew this part by hand, a faster option is to sew around the front of the quilt using a narrow zigzag stitch centered over the previous seam. This should catch the edge of your binding that's folded to the back, anchoring it in place. Check the back of your quilt occasionally to make sure this is happening.

The Quilts!

Now that you've learned all the essential skills needed to make a quilt, here are some simple quilt projects to try! Refer back to the Quilt Anatomy section (page 35) if you need a refresher on the basic components of a quilt and how they're made, and go back to the previous chapter to brush up on the fundamental techniques as needed.

The projects in this book are rated to reflect the complexity of the techniques used, as well as the overall time needed to create the projects. All of these quilts are completely approachable for beginners or confident beginners, but some are certainly easier than others. Note that with many of the quilts, the size of the project increases the difficulty. If you choose to make a small project bigger, the difficulty will likely increase, and if you scale down a larger project, you'll find it's much more manageable. Here's how the rating works.

Ideal for first-time quilters. Basic sewing experience is needed, but the designs here are perfect for sewers who have yet to put together all the steps in assembling a whole quilt.

These quilts are aimed at sewers who have put together one or two quilts already and are prepared to move on to something more challenging.

The most difficult quilts in this book will be suitable for sewers who have most of the quilting basics pretty well in hand and can manage unexpected hiccups fairly easily.

In addition to the difficulty rating and techniques used, each project will indicate the materials and tools you'll need so you know what to shop for during your next trip to the quilt store. Then you'll be instructed about creating the patchwork from your fabric. The patchwork will be created using either pattern pieces and templates found in the book or squares and strips that you can easily cut without patterns.

You'll find loads of photographs and illustrations to help you with every step of the process, so you're guaranteed a gorgeous project every time!

Coming Up Crosses Wall Hanging

Difficulty:

Techniques:
Rotary cutting (page 34)
Piecing (page 36)
Hanging sleeves

Featured size: Wall hanging
(36½" x 18½" [92.7 x 47cm]), see page 70
for additional sizes

Suggested fabrics: Quilting cotton,
flannel, linen, poplin

Tools: Quilter's toolkit (see page 19)

Materials

Fabric		Yardage
Color 1		¼ yd. (0.3m)
Color 2		¼ yd. (0.3m)
Color 3		¼ yd. (0.3m)
Color 4		¼ yd. (0.3m)
Color 5		¼ yd. (0.3m)
Color 6		⅛ yd. (0.2m)
Backing fabric		1 yd. (1m)
Binding fabric		⅓ yd. (0.4m)
45" (114.5cm)-wide batting		¾ yd. (0.7m)

This small but eye-catching wall hanging is covered with a fresh and modern pattern of plus signs. With a monochromatic ombré color scheme, it will give your home a wonderfully artful feel. This design would work just as well with lots of other color schemes. A pop of contrasting color from a complementary color scheme is sure to make a standout piece.

PRECUT PERFECT!
I used a jelly roll of blue batik for this quilt. The ombré theme of the jelly roll made it incredibly easy to get the look I wanted.

Cutting plan

Set aside all of the backing fabrics and batting for the time being. Gather the patchwork fabrics and, following the rotary cutting instructions on page 34, cut the following fabric strips along the width of the fabric yardage. Then subcut the strips as directed below. The fabrics have been assigned a number based on color and a letter based on size. Sort your cut pieces by color for easy assembly, labeling them with a sticky note if desired.

From Color 1 cut:

3 strips: 2½" (6.4cm) x width of fabric; subcut into:

- 3 squares, 2½" x 2½" [6.4 x 6.4cm] (1A)

- 1 rectangle, 4½" x 2½" [11.4 x 6.4cm] (1B)

- 1 rectangle, 6½" x 2½" [16.5 x 6.4cm] (1C)

- 4 rectangles, 8 ½" x 2 ½" [21.6 x 6.4cm] (1D)

- 3 rectangles, 10½" x 2½" [26.7 x 6.4cm] (1E)

- 1 rectangle, 12 ½" x 2½" [31.8 x 6.4cm] (1F)

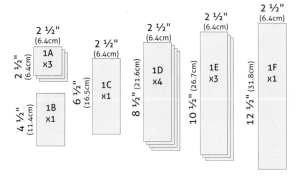

From Color 2 cut:

2 strips: 2½" (6.4cm) x width of fabric; subcut into:

- 11 squares, 2½" x 2½" [6.4 x 6.4cm] (2A)

- 5 rectangles, 6½" x 2½" [16.5 x 6.4cm] (2C)

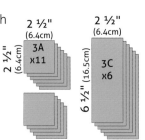

From Color 3 cut:

2 strips: 2½" (6.4cm) x width of fabric; subcut into:

- 11 squares, 2½" x 2½" [6.4 x 6.4cm] (3A)

- 6 rectangles, 6½" x 2½" [16.5 x 6.4cm] (3B)

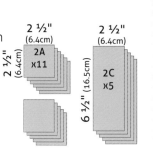

From Color 4 cut:

2 strips: 2½" (6.4cm) x width of fabric; subcut into:

- 12 squares, 2½" x 2½" [6.4 x 6.4cm] (4A)

- 2 rectangles, 4 ½" x 2 ½" [11.4 x 6.4cm] (4B)

- 4 rectangles, 6½" x 2½" [16.5 x 6.4cm] (4C)

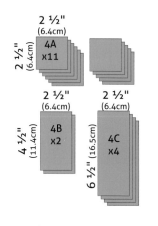

From Color 5 cut:

2 strips: 2½" (6.4cm) x width of fabric; subcut into:

- 9 squares, 2½" x 2½" [6.4 x 6.4cm] (5A)

- 1 rectangle, 4½" x 2½" [11.4 x 6.4cm] (5B)

- 4 rectangles, 6½" x 2½" [16.5 x 6.4cm] (5C)

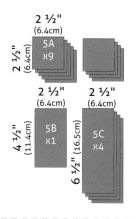

From Color 6 cut:

1 strip: 2½" (6.4cm) x width of fabric; subcut into:

- 6 squares, 2½" x 2½" [6.4 x 6.4cm] (6A)

- 1 rectangle, 4½" x 2½" [11.4 x 6.4cm] (6B)

- 1 rectangle, 6½" x 2½" [16.5 x 6.4cm] (6C)

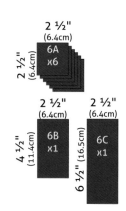

Row

6B	5A	6A	5C	4A	3C	4A	1D		4B	1

6A		5C	4A	5A	4C	3A	2A	1E	2A	4A	2
5A	6A	5A	4C		3A	4A	1A	2C	1C	2C	3
6C		3A	4A	3C	1B	2A	1D	3A	2A	3A	4
5A	6A	3C	2A	3A	1E	2A	1A	3C		4A	5
5B	4A	3A	2C	1D	2C	4A	3A	4B	6
5A	4C	1A	2A	1E	3A	2A	4C	5A	4A	7
2A	3A	4A	1F	2A	3C	5A	4A	5C	8
3C	2A	1D	2C	3A	5C	6A	5A	6A	9

Figure A.

Piecing

Use a scant ¼" (6mm) seam allowance for all seams. Press seam allowances open or to the side as desired; mine are pressed open.

Figure A

1. Sew the first row of fabric pieces together following Row 1 (the one at the top) of Figure A. Use the assigned numbers and letters to select the proper fabric squares and rectangles.
2. Assemble each row as shown in Figure A until all rows are sewn.
3. Then sew the rows together in the order shown in Figure A.

Assembly

4. Trim a 36" x 6" (91.4 x 15.2cm) rectangle off one edge of the backing fabric; set this aside for the hanging sleeve.
5. Layer the remaining backing fabric (right side down), batting, and quilt top (right side up) on top of one another in a sandwich (see page 50).
6. Quilt the wall hanging as desired (page 48).
7. Trim off the excess batting and backing fabric.

USING A DESIGN WALL

Because all the pieces in this wall hanging need to follow Figure A exactly, it's helpful to have a space to spread out all your pieces so you can see them all together. Not everyone has a huge table to work on, so a design wall is a great option. Pin a large piece of batting or flannel-backed tablecloth to the largest empty wall you have. The fuzzy surface of the fabric will allow you to stick thin fabrics like cotton on it with ease. Now you can lay out rows or an entire quilt exactly as you plan to sew it.

Finishing

1 **Hem the sleeve.** Turn under and iron the short edges of the trimmed 36" x 6" (91.5 x 15cm) rectangle by ½" (1.5cm); repeat this one more time and sew the folds in place to complete the double fold hems.

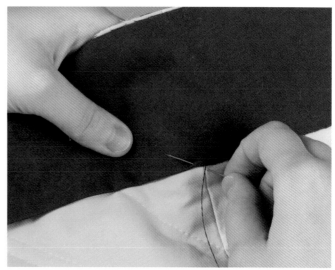

2 **Attach the folded sleeve.** Fold the piece of fabric in half lengthwise, wrong sides together, and center it at the top of your quilt, aligning its raw edges with the raw edge of the quilt. Hand sew the fold in place for an invisible join or, if it goes with your quilting, machine stitch this fold in place.

3 **Bind the quilt.** Following the directions for binding (page 58), bind the edges of the quilt. To display your quilt, slide a curtain rod or wooden dowel through the sleeve and hang with hooks on either side.

QUILT IT!

This quilt has a straight-line quilting treatment done with a walking foot. Because the cross motif uses mostly horizontal and vertical lines, I used zigzagging echo quilting (easily done with masking tape) across the piece to break up the monotony without being too jarring. The zigzag pattern also creates a sense of movement going across the quilt to reinforce the ombré color scheme.

Would you like to make this wall hanging in a larger size? It can be done with a little extra effort. To work with this asymmetrical pattern, simply repeat Steps 1–3 of the Piecing section to make one block. For the next block, repeat Steps 1 and 2 of the Piecing section to create the strips, but for Step 3, rotate the strips 180 degrees before stitching them together (see Figure B). This creates a reflection effect that will look fabulous when you stitch the blocks together.

Note that the baby size quilt consists of three of the wall quilts attached together. For twin, full, and queen/king, the sizes of the squares and rectangles in the block have been changed. The construction method is the same, but it'll be far less challenging working with larger squares than those required for the wall hanging.

Color variations: Would you like to make this quilt in a different color palette? Check out the options here to spark your creativity.

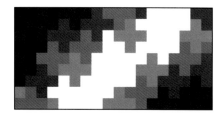

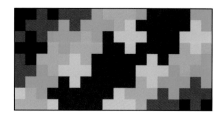

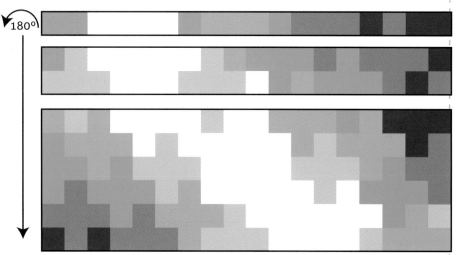

180°

Figure B: To get a perfectly reflected block, flip each row 180° before joining them.

Baby -
36 ½" x 54 ½"
(92.7 x 138.4cm)

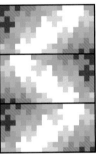

Full - 81 ½" x 81 ½"
(207 x 207cm)

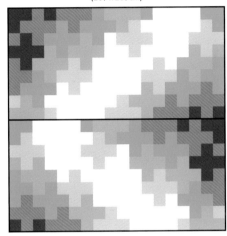

Twin - 54 ½" x 81 ½"
(138.4 x 207cm)

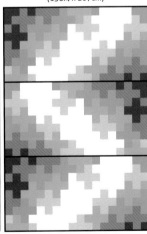

Queen/King - 99 ½" x 99 ½"
(252.7 x 252.7cm)

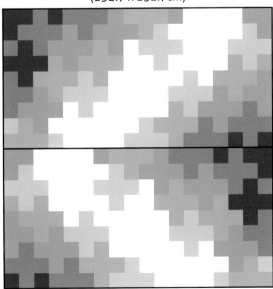

	Baby	Twin	Full	Queen/King
Finished size	36½" x 54½" (92.7 x 138.4cm)	54½" x 81½" (138.4 x 207cm)	81½" x 81½" (207 x 207cm)	99½" x 99½" (252.7 x 252.7cm)
Block configuration	1 block x 3 blocks (3 total)	1 block x 3 blocks (3 total)	1 block x 2 blocks (2 total)	1 block x 2 blocks (2 total)
Materials needed				
Color 1	⅔ yd. (0.7m)	1⅓ yd. (1.3m)	2¼ yd. (2.1m)	3½ yd. (3.3m)
Color 2	½ yd. (0.5m)	¾ yd. (0.7m)	1¼ yd. (1.2m)	1⅔ yd. (1.6m)
Color 3	½ yd. (0.5m)	1 yd. (1m)	1⅓ yd. (1.3m)	1¾ yd. (1.7m)
Color 4	½ yd. (0.5m)	1 yd. (1m)	1¼ yd. (1.2m)	1¾ yd. (1.7m)
Color 5	½ yd. (0.5m)	⅔ yd. (0.7m)	1 yd. (1m)	1½ yd. (1.4m)
Color 6	¼ yd. (0.3m)	⅓ yd. (0.4m)	½ yd. (0.5m)	¾ yd. (0.7m)
Batting	45" x 63" (114.3 x 160cm)	63" x 90" (160 x 228.6cm)	90" x 90" (228.6 x 228.6cm)	108" x 108" (274.3 x 274.3cm)
Backing	2 yd. (1.9m) of 60" (152.4cm) wide backing	2 yd. (1.9m) of 106" (269.2cm) wide backing	2⅔ yd. (2.5m) of 106" (269.2cm) wide backing	3¼ yd. (3m) of 118" (299.7cm) wide backing
Binding	½ yd. (0.5m)	⅔ yd. (0.7m)	¾ yd. (0.7m)	1 yd. (1m)
Color 1				
Strips to cut:	9 strips: 2½" (6.4cm) x width of fabric	13 strips: 3½" (8.9cm) x width of fabric	15 strips: 5" (12.7cm) x width of fabric	19 strips: 6" (15.2cm) x width of fabric
Subcut into:	9 squares: 2½" x 2½" (1A) (6.4 x 6.4cm)	9 squares: 3½" x 3½" (1A) (8.9 x 8.9cm)	6 squares: 5" x 5" (1A) (12.7 x 12.7cm)	6 squares: 6" x 6" (1A) (15.2 x 15.2cm)
	3 rectangles: 4½" x 2½" (1B) (11.4 x 6.4cm)	3 rectangles: 6½" x 3½" (1B) (16.5 x 8.9cm)	2 rectangles: 9½" x 5" (1B) (24.1 x 12.7cm)	2 rectangles: 11½" x 6" (1B) (29.2 x 15.2cm)
	3 rectangles: 6½" x 2½" (1C) (16.5 x 6.4cm)	3 rectangles: 9½" x 3½" (1C) (24.1 x 8.9cm)	2 rectangles: 14" x 5" (1C) (35.6 x 12.7cm)	2 rectangles: 17" x 6" (1C) (43.2 x 15.2cm)
	12 rectangles: 8½" x 2½" (1D) (21.6 x 6.4cm)	12 rectangles: 12½" x 3½" (1D) (31.8 x 8.9cm)	8 rectangles: 18½" x 5" (1D) (47 x 12.7cm)	8 rectangles: 22½" x 6" (1D) (57.2 x 15.2cm)
	9 rectangles: 10½" x 2½" (1E) (26.7 x 6.4cm)	9 rectangles: 15½" x 3½" (1E) (39.4 x 8.9cm)	6 rectangles: 23" x 5" (1E) (58.4 x 12.7cm)	6 rectangles: 28" x 6" (1E) (71.1 x 15.2cm)
	3 rectangles: 12½" x 2½" (1F) (31.8 x 6.4cm)	3 rectangles: 18½" x 3½" (1F) (47 x 8.9cm)	2 rectangles: 27½" x 5" (1F) (69.9 x 12.7cm)	2 rectangles: 33½" x 6" (1F) (85.1 x 15.2cm)
Color 2				
Strips to cut:	5 strips: 2½" (6.4cm) x width of fabric	7 strips: 3½" (8.9cm) x width of fabric	8 strips: 5" (12.7cm) x width of fabric	9 strips: 6" (15.2cm) x width of fabric
Subcut into:	33 squares: 2½" x 2½" (2A) (6.4 x 6.4cm)	33 squares: 3½" x 3½" (2A) (8.9 x 8.9cm)	22 squares: 5" x 5" (2A) (12.7 x 12.7cm)	22 squares: 6" x 6" (2A) (15.2 x 15.2cm)
	15 rectangles: 6½" x 2½" (2C) (16.5 x 6.4cm)	15 rectangles: 9½" x 3½" (2C) (24.1 x 8.9cm)	10 rectangles: 14" x 5" (2C) (35.6 x 12.7cm)	10 rectangles: 17" x 6" (2C) (43.2 x 15.2cm)

	Baby	Twin	Full	Queen/King
Color 3				
Strips to cut:	6 strips: 2½" (6.4cm) x width of fabric	8 strips: 3½" (8.9cm) x width of fabric	9 strips: 5" (12.7cm) x width of fabric	10 strips: 6" (15.2cm) x width of fabric
Subcut into:	33 squares: 2½" x 2½" (3A) (6.4 x 6.4cm)	33 squares: 3½" x 3½" (3A) (8.9 x 8.9cm)	22 squares: 5" x 5" (3A) (12.7 x 12.7cm)	22 squares: 6" x 6" (3A) (15.2 x 15.2cm)
	18 rectangles: 6½" x 2½" (3C) (16.5 x 6.4cm)	18 rectangles: 9½" x 3½" (3C) (24.1 x 8.9cm)	12 rectangles: 14" x 5" (3C) (35.6 x 12.7cm)	12 rectangles: 17" x 6" (3C) (43.2 x 15.2cm)
Color 4				
Strips to cut:	5 strips: 2½" (6.4cm) x width of fabric	8 strips: 3½" (8.9cm) x width of fabric	8 strips: 5" (12.7cm) x width of fabric	10 strips: 6" (15.2cm) x width of fabric
Subcut into:	36 squares: 2½" x 2½" (4A) (6.4 x 6.4cm)	36 squares: 3½" x 3½" (4A) (8.9 x 8.9cm)	24 squares: 5" x 5" (4A) (12.7 x 12.7cm)	24 squares: 6" x 6" (4A) (15.2 x 15.2cm)
	6 rectangles: 4½" x 2½" (4B) (11.4 x 6.4cm)	6 rectangles: 6½" x 3½" (4B) (16.5 x 8.9cm)	4 rectangles: 9½" x 5" (4B) (24.1 x 12.7cm)	4 rectangles: 11½" x 6" (4B) (29.2 x 15.2cm)
	12 rectangles: 6½" x 2½" (4C) (16.5 x 6.4cm)	12 rectangles: 9½" x 3½" (4C) (24.1 x 8.9cm)	8 rectangles: 14" x 5" (4C) (35.6 x 12.7cm)	8 rectangles: 17" x 6" (4C) (43.2 x 15.2cm)
Color 5				
Strips to cut:	5 strips: 2½" (6.4cm) x width of fabric	6 strips: 3½" (8.9cm) x width of fabric	7 strips: 5" (12.7cm) x width of fabric	8 strips: 6" (15.2cm) x width of fabric
Subcut into:	27 squares: 2½" x 2½" (5A) (6.4 x 6.4cm)	27 squares: 3½" x 3½" (5A) (8.9 x 8.9cm)	18 squares: 5" x 5" (5A) (12.7 x 12.7cm)	18 squares: 6" x 6" (5A) (15.2 x 15.2cm)
	3 rectangles: 4½" x 2½" (5B) (11.4 x 6.4cm)	3 rectangles: 6½" x 3½" (5B) (16.5 x 8.9cm)	2 rectangles: 9½" x 5" (5B) (24.1 x 12.7cm)	2 rectangles: 11½" x 6" (5B) (29.2 x 15.2cm)
	12 rectangles: 6½" x 2½" (5C) (16.5 x 6.4cm)	12 rectangles: 9½" x 3½" (5C) (24.1 x 8.9cm)	8 rectangles: 14" x 5" (5C) (35.6 x 12.7cm)	8 rectangles: 17" x 7" (5C) (43.2 x 15.2cm)
Color 6				
Strips to cut:	2 strips: 2½" (6.4cm) x width of fabric	3 strips: 3½" (8.9cm) x width of fabric	3 strips: 5" (12.5cm) x width of fabric	4 strips: 6" (15.2cm) x width of fabric
Subcut into:	18 squares: 2½" x 2½" (6A) (6.4 x 6.4cm)	18 squares: 3½" x 3½" (6A) (8.9 x 8.9cm)	12 squares: 5" x 5" (6A) (12.7 x 12.7cm)	12 squares: 6" x 6" (6A) (15.2 x 15.2cm)
	3 rectangles: 4½" x 2½" (6B) (11.4 x 6.4cm)	3 rectangles: 6½" x 3½" (6B) (16.5 x 8.9cm)	2 rectangles: 9½" x 5" (6B) (24.1 x 12.7cm)	2 rectangles: 11½" x 6" (6B) (29.2 x 15.2cm)
	3 rectangles: 6½" x 2½" (6C) (16.5 x 6.4cm)	3 rectangles: 9½" x 3½" (6C) (24.1 x 8.9cm)	2 rectangles: 14" x 5" (6C) (35.6 x 12.7cm)	2 rectangles: 17" x 6" (6C) (43.2 x 15.2cm)

Cozy Clamshell Rug

Difficulty:

Techniques:
Rotary cutting (page 34)
Piecing (page 36)
Raw edge appliqué
Making templates (page 76)

Featured size: Rug (29½" x 20" [74.9 x 50.8cm]), see page 80 for additional sizes

Suggested fabrics: Quilting cotton, flannel, linen, poplin, terry cloth

Tools
- Quilter's toolkit (see page 19)
- Template-making material (see Mini Lesson: Making Templates, page 76)
- Basting spray

Materials

Fabric	Yardage
Background fabric	⅔ yd. (0.7m)
Backing fabric	⅔ yd. (0.7m)
45" (114.5cm)-wide batting (preferably an all-natural batting)	⅔ yd. (0.7m)
Varying prints	8 fat eighths

This soft and absorbent rug is made with a raw edge appliqué method that leaves all the edges especially fuzzy. If you wanted to avoid the raw edges, you could also use the fusible web or freezer paper appliqué techniques on pages 43 and 45. I used terry cloth for the backing fabric, making it perfect for the bathroom. The blocks are made from a kind of quilt-as-you-go method, where every joining seam is left exposed to add to the fluffy look. This technique can be used on other quilt blocks as well if you particularly like its cozy feel.

Cutting plan

Following the instructions for Making Templates at the right, make a template of the pattern on page 79. Set aside until needed. Following the rotary cutting instructions on page 34, cut the following fabric strips along the width of the fabric yardage. Then subcut the strips as directed below.

From the background fabric cut:

2 strips: 10½" (26.7cm) x width of fabric; subcut into:

- 6 squares, 10½" x 10½" [26.7 x 26.7cm]

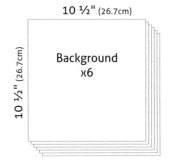

From the backing fabric cut:

2 strips: 10½" (26.7cm) x width of fabric; subcut into:

- 6 squares, 10½" x 10½" [26.7 x 26.7cm]

From the batting cut:

2 strips: 9½" (24.1cm) x width of fabric; subcut into:

- 6 squares, 10" x 10" [25.4 x 25.4cm]

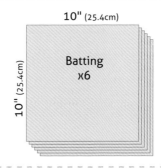

From the fat eighths cut:

10–15 appliqué pieces from each fat eighth, using the template (80–120 total). I used 96 pieces (12 from each fat eighth), but you may want extra.

10-15 shapes per fabric

MINI LESSON: MAKING TEMPLATES

A quilting template is a kind of pattern used especially for pieces that need to be repeated several times over. You can make a paper template from freezer paper and iron it onto your fabric for tracing, or you can make one from plastic. Template plastic is available for sale at quilt shops, but you can also source your own from thin, soft plastic around the house, such as the lids of coffee cans, margarine tubs, and other food products. Simply trace the desired shape onto the plastic and cut it out with craft scissors. You can then trace around the template onto your cloth with a fabric marker to easily create as many of the same shape as you like.

Making templates. Templates are a quick way of tracing a shape outline over and over again. Buy template plastic at your local quilt shop, or recycle soft plastic from food packaging.

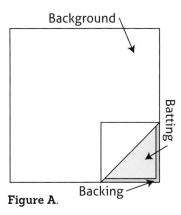

Figure A.

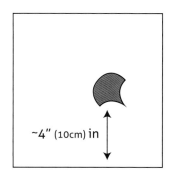

Figure B.

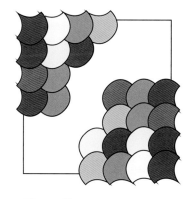

Figure C.

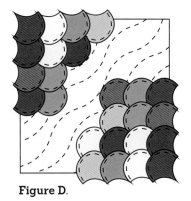

Figure D.

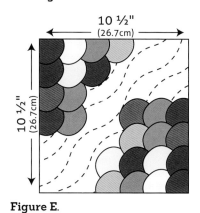

Figure E.

Assembly

1. Lay out a square of batting and spray it lightly with basting spray. Press the batting onto the wrong side of a square of backing fabric. Spray the side of the batting that's face up with more basting spray, and press a square of background fabric on top of it, right side up (Figure A).

2. Use basting spray to attach one of the appliqué pieces onto the background fabric, positioning it about 4" (10.2cm) in from the bottom edge of the square with the point aimed toward the bottom right corner (Figure B).

3. Use basting spray to layer additional appliqué pieces over the first one, positioning each so the new pieces cover the points of the previous ones. Repeat in a pattern of your choosing until you reach the bottom and right edges, covering the corner. Repeat Steps 2–3 on the opposite corner of the square of background fabric (Figure C).

4. Anchor the appliqué in place by sewing along the top curved edge of each piece. Stitch about ⅛"–¼" (3–6mm) away from the raw edge, making a scalloped shape as you move from one shape to the next. The edges are left raw for a casual look.

5. Quilt the middle of the block between the sections of appliqué as desired (Figure D).

6. Referring to Figure E, trim off and discard any appliqué bits spilling over the edges of the block so it's 10½" x 10½" (26.7 x 26.7cm). Topstitch around the perimeter of the block, ½" (1.2cm) from the edge. Repeat Steps 1–6 five more times to create six blocks total.

Quilting Simplified

77

QUILT IT!

The stitching along the curved edge of each scallop piece serves as part of the finished quilting and outlines each appliqué piece nicely. Upon seeing the layout of the scallops in opposing corners, I thought of a flowing stream with pebbles on each bank, so it felt only natural to do gentle waves (with a walking foot) going down the middle of each block. So simple, and it works with the pattern!

Figure F.

Photo G.

Photo H.

7. Sew two blocks together along one side with back sides facing and using a ½" (1.3cm) seam allowance. Add a third block to one end, creating a row of three blocks. In the same manner, create a second row from the remaining blocks. Press the seams in opposing directions.

8. With back sides facing, stitch the two rows of blocks together along the long edge using a ½" (1.3cm) seam allowance; make sure the opposing seam allowances of each row are nested together (Figure F).

9. Carefully clip about ⅜" (1cm) into the fabric of each seam allowance every ½" (1.3cm) or so to create fringe along the seams and outer edges of the rug (Photo G).

10. Run the rug through the washer and dryer to enhance the fraying of the edges. Trim any excess threads (Photo H).

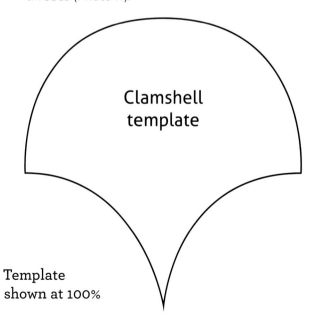

Clamshell template

Template shown at 100%

Just My Size: Cozy Clamshell Rug

Want to turn this rug into a quilt? Simply create the necessary number of blocks to reach your desired size. Refer to the chart for the material and block requirements and assemble the quilt following the instructions for the rug.

Color variations: Would you like to make this quilt in a different color palette? Check out the options here to spark your creativity.

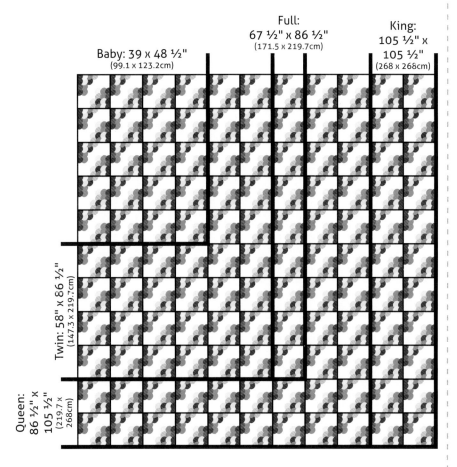

Baby: 39 x 48 ½"
(99.1 x 123.2cm)

Full:
67 ½" x 86 ½"
(171.5 x 219.7cm)

King:
105 ½" x
105 ½"
(268 x 268cm)

Twin: 58" x 86 ½"
(147.3 x 219.7cm)

Queen:
86 ½" x
105 ½"
(219.7 x
268cm)

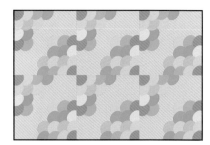

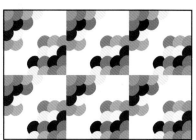

Quilt layout: Use the number of blocks indicated by the illustration and the chart to construct your quilt to size.

Cozy Clamshell Rug

	Baby	**Twin**	**Full**	**Queen**	**King**
Finished size	39" x 48½" (99.1 x 123.2cm)	58" x 86½" (147.3 x 219.7cm)	67½" x 86½" (171.5 x 219.7cm)	86½" x 105½" (219.7 x 268cm)	105½" x 105½" (268 x 268cm)
Block configuration	4 blocks x 5 blocks (20 total)	6 blocks x 9 blocks (54 total)	7 blocks x 9 blocks (63 total)	9 blocks x 11 blocks (99 total)	11 blocks x 11 blocks (121 total)
Materials needed					
At least five coordinating focus fabrics, totaling:	1½ yd. (1.4m)	3¼ yd. (3m)	3¾ yd. (3.5m)	5¾ yd. (5.3m)	7 yd. (6.4m)
Background fabrics (42" [106.7cm]wide)	1½ yd. (1.4m)	4¼ yd. (3.9m)	4¾ yd. (4.4m)	7⅓ yd. (6.8m)	9¼ yd. (8.5m)
Batting (45" [114.3cm] wide)	1⅓ yd. (1.3m)	3¾ yd. (3.5m)	4¼ yd. (3.9m)	6⅔ yd. (6.1m)	8¼ yd. (7.6m)
Backing (42" [106.7cm] wide)	1½ yd. (1.4m)	4¼ yd. (3.9m)	4¾ yd. (4.4m)	7⅓ yd. (6.8m)	9¼ yd. (8.5m)
Background fabrics					
Strips to cut:	5 strips: 10½" (26.7cm) x width of fabric	14 strips: 10½" (26.7cm) x width of fabric	16 strips: 10½" (26.7cm) x width of fabric	25 strips: 10½" (26.7cm) x width of fabric	31 strips: 10½" (26.7cm) x width of fabric
Subcut into:	20 squares: 10½" x 10½" (26.7 x 26.7cm)	54 squares: 10½" x 10½" (26.7 x 26.7cm)	63 squares: 10½" x 10½" (26.7 x 26.7cm)	99 squares: 10½" x 10½" (26.7 x 26.7cm)	121 squares: 10½" x 10½" (26.7 x 26.7cm)
Backing fabric					
Strips to cut:	5 strips: 10½" (26.7cm) x width of fabric	14 strips: 10½" (26.7cm) x width of fabric	16 strips: 10½" (26.7cm) x width of fabric	25 strips: 10½" (26.7cm) x width of fabric	31 strips: 10½" (26.7cm) x width of fabric
Subcut into:	20 squares: 10½" x 10½" (26.7 x 26.7cm)	54 squares: 10½" x 10½" (26.7 x 26.7cm)	63 squares: 10½" x 10½" (26.7 x 26.7cm)	99 squares: 10½" x 10½" (26.7 x 26.7cm)	121 squares: 10½" x 10½" (26.7 x 26.7cm)
Batting					
Strips to cut:	5 strips: 9½" (24.1cm) x width of fabric	14 strips: 9½" (24.1cm) x width of fabric	16 strips: 9½" (24.1cm) x width of fabric	25 strips: 9½" (24.1cm) x width of fabric	31 strips: 9½" (24.1cm) x width of fabric
Subcut into:	20 squares: 9½" x 9½" (24.1 x 24.1cm)	54 squares: 9½" x 9½" (24.1 x 24.1cm)	63 squares: 9½" x 9½" (24.1 x 24.1cm)	99 squares: 9½" x 9½" (24.1 x 24.1cm)	121 squares: 9½" x 9½" (24.1 x 24.1cm)
Appliqué pieces					
Pieces to cut:	400 pieces, cut from the various fabrics	1080 pieces, cut from the various fabrics	1260 pieces, cut from the various fabrics	1980 pieces, cut from the various fabrics	2420 pieces, cut from the various fabrics

Cheater Hexie Quilt

Difficulty:

Techniques:
Rotary cutting (page 34)
Piecing (page 36)
Making templates (page 76)

Featured size: Lap (44⅝" x 44¾" [113.3 x 113.7cm]), see page 88 for additional sizes

Suggested fabrics: Quilting cotton, flannel, linen, poplin, voile, chambray

Tools
- Quilter's toolkit (see page 19)
- Template-making material (see Mini Lesson: Making Templates, page 76)

Materials

Fabric	Yardage
At least three varying focus fabrics	1¼ yd. (1.2m) total
Background fabric	2⅓ yd. (2.2m)
Batting	53" x 53" (134.6 x 134.6cm)
60" (152.5cm)-wide backing fabric	1⅔ yd. (1.6m)
Binding fabric	½ yd. (0.5m)

Hexagon quilts are so popular with modern quilters! There are loads of ways to piece hexagons: hand-sewn English paper piecing, machine sewn Y-seams, triangles, or trapezoids. My method takes all the guesswork out of hexagons by using a simple template. The secret lies in the honeycomb border, which adds a beautiful design element while eliminating Y-seams or any color planning. Note that you could also use the template as a foundation piecing pattern. If you follow the technique on page 40, using the corresponding fabrics on each section of the template, you have another option for creating this project.

PRECUT PERFECT!
The template for this project works wonderfully with 10" (25.4cm) charm squares and would replace all the focus fabrics you need. Get enough charm squares to equal the number of hexagons in your quilt—26 for the lap quilt pictured here.

Cutting plan

Following the instructions for Making Templates on page 76, make a template of the pattern at the right. Set aside until needed. Set aside the backing fabric and batting for later use; for now, gather all of the patchwork fabrics. Following the rotary cutting instructions on page 34, cut your fabric strips along the width of the fabric yardage. Make any subcuts as instructed, then sort and pile your fabrics according to letters A through E, labeling them with a sticky note as necessary.

From the focus fabrics cut:

6 strips: 7" (17.8cm) x width of fabric; subcut into:
• 26 squares, 7⅞" x 7" (20 x 17.8cm)

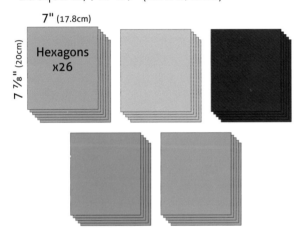

7" (17.8cm)

7 ⅞" (20cm)

Hexagons x26

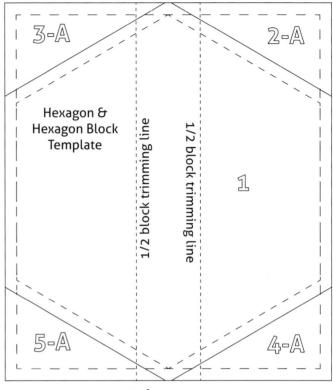

Hexagon & Hexagon Block Template

3-A 2-A

1/2 block trimming line

1/2 block trimming line

1

5-A 4-A

Enlarge 200%

From the background fabric cut:

13 strips: 2½" (6.4cm) x width of fabric; subcut into:
• 104 rectangles: 5" x 2½" [12.7 x 6.4cm] (A)

5 strips: 2⅜" (6cm) x width of fabric; subcut into:
• 22 rectangles: 7⅞" x 2⅜" [20 x 6cm] (B)

2 strips: 7⅞" (20cm) x width of fabric; subcut into:
• 1 rectangle, 25⅝" x 7⅞" [65.1 x 20cm] (C)
• 2 rectangles: 13" x 7⅞" [33 x 20cm] (D)
• 1 rectangle: 8⅞" x 7⅞" [22.5 x 20cm] (E)

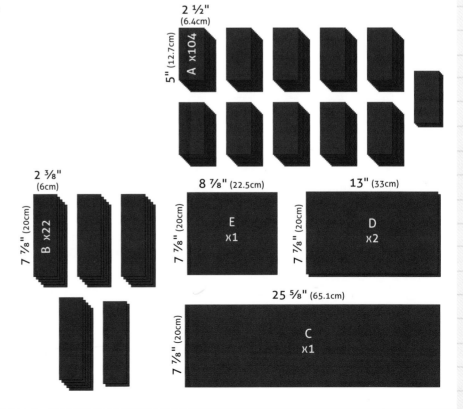

2 ½" (6.4cm)

5" (12.7cm) A x104

2 ⅜" (6cm)

7 ⅞" (20cm) B x22

8 ⅞" (22.5cm)

7 ⅞" (20cm) E x1

13" (33cm)

7 ⅞" (20cm) D x2

25 ⅝" (65.1cm)

7 ⅞" (20cm) C x1

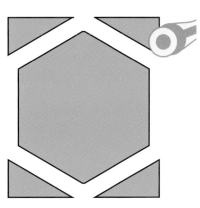

Figure A.

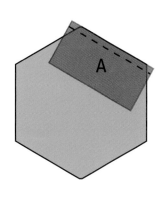

Figure B.

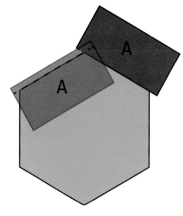

Figure C.

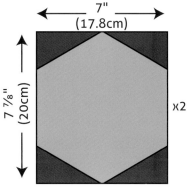

Figure D.

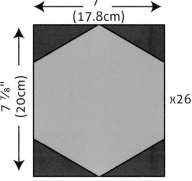

Figure E.

Piecing

Use a scant ¼" (6mm) for all seams. Press seam allowances open or to the side as desired; mine are pressed open.

1. Place the template over each of the 26 rectangles cut from the focus fabrics and trim off the excess corners, turning each rectangle into a hexagon (Figure A).

2. Align the long edge of one of the A rectangles along the top right edge of the hexagon with right sides facing. Sew them together with a scant ¼" (6mm) seam allowance (Figure B).

3. Press the background fabric away from the hexagon and, much as in Step 2, stitch another A rectangle to the top left edge of the hexagon (Figure C). Press as before.

4. Stitch two more A rectangles to the bottom edges of the hexagon, opposite the rectangles added in Steps 2 and 3. This will create a hexagon with sloppy corners on the top and bottom. Press. As shown in Figure D, and carefully noting the orientation of the points of the hexagon in the illustration, trim it down to a rectangle 7" x 7⅞" (17.8 x 20cm).

5. To complete all the hexagons for the quilt layout, repeat Steps 2 to 4 twenty-five more times to create 26 rectangles total.

6. In order to create the right tiling pattern for the hexagons, some rows of the quilt have a shorter block at the end to maintain the correct spacing. On the template pattern you'll see two sets of dashed cutting lines; trim two of the blocks along these cutting lines, creating four halves total (Figure E). Discard the narrow center pieces, and label the remaining pieces F.

Quilting Simplified

85

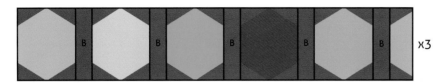

Figure F.

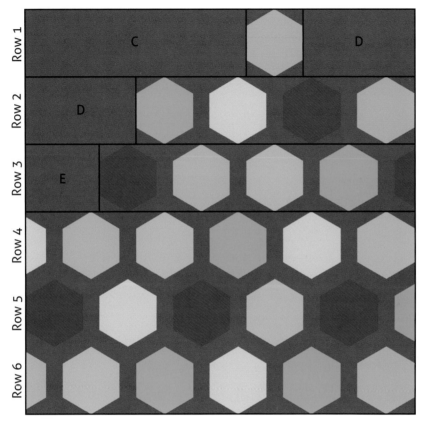

Figure G.

7. Following Figure F, and taking careful note of the orientation of the hexagons, create a row of hexagons by sewing five hexagons with four sashing rectangles (B) in between. Then add one more sashing rectangle (B), then a half hexagon (F) at the end. Repeat this twice more to create three rows total. (You'll end up using these for rows 4, 5, and 6 in the next step.)

8. To create rows 1, 2, and 3, follow Figure G, using the large background rectangles (C–E) in conjunction with the whole and half hexagons (F) and sashing strips (B). Then sew all the rows together in order as indicated in the illustration.

Finishing

Sandwich the quilt top, batting, and backing (page 50). Quilt the layers as desired (page 48), and bind the edges (page 58) to finish.

QUILT IT!

With this quilt, I felt inclined to simply highlight the hexagons and the honeycomb border with the quilting. I stuck to simple outline quilting around each hexagon, while inside each hexagon, I echoed the outlines at various distances for some diversity. Using the guidelines on my walking foot made this very manageable.

Just My Size: Cheater Hexie Quilt

Would you like to make this quilt in a different size? Simply repeat more of the hexagon blocks to get the size that you need. Refer to this chart for the proper sizes and create the quilt as described in the instructions. To create your own composition of blank space and hexagons, you can simply replace some of the hexagon pieces with rectangles from the background fabric without having to do any math.

Color variations: Would you like to make this quilt in a different color palette? Check out the options here to spark your creativity.

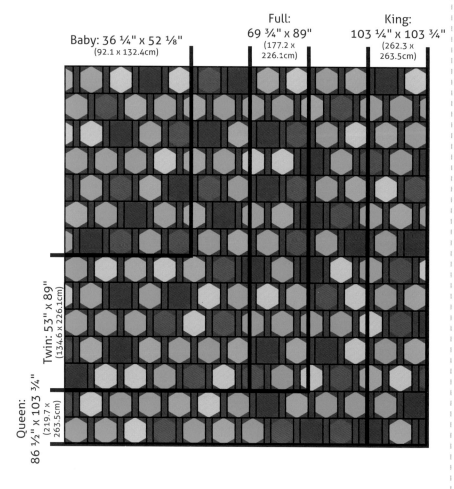

Baby: 36 ¼" x 52 ⅛" (92.1 x 132.4cm)

Full: 69 ¾" x 89" (177.2 x 226.1cm)

King: 103 ¼" x 103 ¾" (262.3 x 263.5cm)

Twin: 53" x 89" (134.6 x 226.1cm)

Queen: 86 ½" x 103 ¾" (219.7 x 263.5cm)

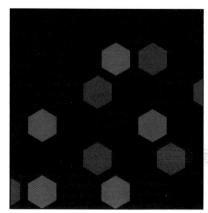

Quilt layout: Use the number of blocks indicated by the illustration and the chart to construct your quilt to size.

Cheater Hexie Quilt

	Baby	Twin	Full	Queen	King
Finished size	36¼" x 52⅛" (92.1 x 132.4cm)	53" x 89" (134.6 x 226.1cm)	69¾" x 89" (177.2 x 226.1cm)	86½" x 103¾" (219.7 x 263.5cm)	103¼" x 103¾" (262.3 x 263.5cm)
Block configuration	4½ blocks x 7 rows (32 total)	6½ blocks x 12 rows (78 total)	8½ blocks x 12 rows (102 total)	10½ blocks x 14 rows (147 total)	12½ blocks x 14 rows (175 total)
Materials needed					
At least three coordinating focus fabrics, totaling:	1½ yd. (1.4m)	3¼ yd. (3m)	4¼ yd. (3.9m)	6 yd. (5.5m)	7 yd. (6.5m)
Background fabrics	1⅔ yd. (1.6m)	3¾ yd. (3.5m)	5 yd. (4.6m)	7 yd. (6.5m)	8½ yd. (7.8m)
Batting	44" x 60" (111.7 x 152.4cm)	61" x 97" (155 x 246.4cm)	78" x 97" (198.1 x 246.4cm)	95" x 112" (241.3 x 284.5cm)	111" x 112" (281.9 x 284.5cm)
Backing	1¾ yd. (1.7m) of 60" (152.4cm) backing	1¾ yd. (1.6m) of 106" (269.2cm) wide backing	2⅓ yd. (2.2m) of 106" (269.2cm) wide backing	2¾ yd. (2.6m) of 118" (299.7cm) wide backing	3¼ yd. (3m) of 118" (299.7cm) wide backing
Binding	½ yd. (0.5m)	⅔ yd. (0.7m)	¾ yd. (0.7m)	1 yd. (1m)	1 yd. (1m)
Focus fabrics					
Strips to cut:	7 strips: 7" (17.8cm) x width of fabric	16 strips: 7" (17.8cm) x width of fabric	21 strips: 7" (17.8cm) x width of fabric	30 strips: 7" (17.8cm) x width of fabric	35 strips: 7" (17.8cm) x width of fabric
Subcut into:	32 rectangles: 7⅞' x 7" (20 x 17.8cm)	78 rectangles: 7⅞" x 7" (20 x 17.8cm)	102 rectangles: 7⅞" x 7" (20 x 17.8cm)	147 rectangles: 7⅞" x 7" (20 x 17.8cm)	175 rectangles: 7⅞" x 7" (20 x 17.8cm)
Background fabrics					
Strips to cut:	16 strips: 2½" (6.4cm) x width of fabric	39 strips: 2½" (6.4cm) x width of fabric	51 strips: 2½" (6.4cm) x width of fabric	74 strips: 2½" (6.4cm) x width of fabric	88 strips: 2½" (6.4cm) x width of fabric
Subcut into:	128 rectangles: 5" x 2½" (A) (12.7 x 6.4cm)	312 rectangles: 5" x 2½" (A) (12.7 x 6.4cm)	408 rectangles: 5" x 2½" (A) (12.7 x 6.4cm)	588 rectangles: 5" x 2½" (A) (12.7 x 6.4cm)	700 rectangles: 5" x 2½" (A) (12.7 x 6.4cm)
Strips to cut:	6 strips: 2⅜" (6cm) x width of fabric	15 strips: 2⅜" (6cm) x width of fabric	20 strips: 2⅜" (6cm) x width of fabric	28 strips: 2⅜" (6cm) x width of fabric	34 strips: 2⅜" (6cm) x width of fabric
Subcut into:	28 rectangles: 7⅞" x 2⅜" (B) (20 x 6cm)	72 rectangles: 7⅞" x 2⅜" (B) (20 x 6cm)	96 rectangles: 7⅞" x 2⅜" (B) (20 x 6cm)	140 rectangles: 7⅞" x 2⅜" (B) (20 x 6cm)	168 rectangles: 7⅞" x 2⅜" (B) (20 x 6cm)

Jeweled Lattice Baby Quilt

Difficulty:

Techniques:
Rotary cutting (page 34)
Piecing (page 36)

Featured size: Baby (37½" x 55½"
[95.3 x 141cm]), see page 96 for
additional sizes

Suggested fabrics: Quilting cotton,
flannel, linen, poplin, voile, chambray

Tools
• Quilter's toolkit (see page 19)

Materials

Fabric	Yardage
Violet and teal fabrics 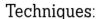	½ yd. (0.5m) each
Seafoam, orange, and magenta fabrics	¼ yd. (0.3m) each
Border fabric	1¼ yd. (1.2m)
Batting	45" x 63" (114.5 x 160cm)
45" (114.5cm)-wide backing fabric	1⅔ yd. (1.6m)
Binding fabric	½ yd. (0.5m)

This quilt is a scrap lover's delight! With loads of tiny pieces surrounded by a bright and fresh lattice border, all of your little fabric scraps will look amazing together. The construction of the quilt is also loads of fun. Not only is it simple, but variety abounds because you can switch and swap out blocks as you go.

PRECUT PERFECT!
The pattern for this project works perfectly with precut strip sets such as jelly rolls. Use them as the focus fabrics to make all the squares—it'll help to cut more squares than you need so you're sure that the right fabrics match up. You can always use the extras to piece the back! For this baby quilt, get a bundle with at least 19 strips to have enough focus fabric. For the twin size you'll need 34 strips; for full, 43; for queen, 55; and if you're making a king-size quilt, get a bundle with at least 67 strips.

Cutting plan

Gather all of the patchwork fabrics for now; set aside all of the backing fabrics and batting for later. Following the rotary cutting instructions on page 34, cut your fabric strips across the width of the fabric yardage. Make any subcuts as instructed, then sort and pile your fabrics separated by letter and color, labeling with a sticky note as necessary.

From the teal and violet fabrics cut:

5 strips from each color: 2½" (6.4cm) x width of fabric (10 total); subcut into:

- 18 rectangles from each color: 3½" x 2½" [8.9 x 6.4cm] (36 total) (A)
- 18 rectangles from each color: 5½" x 2½" [14 x 6.4cm] (36 total) (B)

From the border fabric cut:

29 strips: 1½" (3.8cm) x width of fabric; subcut into:

- 72 rectangles: 2½" x 1½" [6.4 x 3.8cm] (D)
- 18 rectangles: 3½" x 1½" [8.9 x 3.8cm] (E)
- 36 rectangles: 5½" x 1½" [14 x 3.8cm] (F)
- 18 rectangles: 6½" x 1½" [16.5 x 3.8cm] (G)
- 21 strips: 17½" x 1½" [44.5 x 3.8cm] (H)
- 4 strips: 37½" x 1½" [95.3 x 3.8cm] (I)

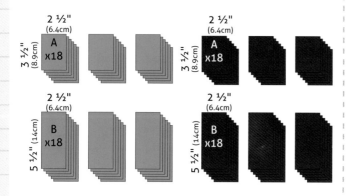

From the seafoam fabric cut:

3 strips: 2½" (6.4cm) x width of fabric; subcut into:

- 18 rectangles: 5½" x 2½" [14 x 6.4cm] (B)

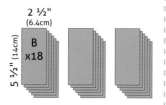

From the orange and magenta fabrics cut:

3 strips from each color: 2½" (6.4cm) x width of fabric (6 total); subcut into:

- 36 squares from each color: 2½" x 2½" [6.4 x 6.4cm] (72 total) (C)

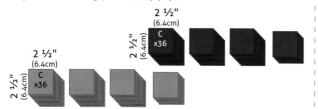

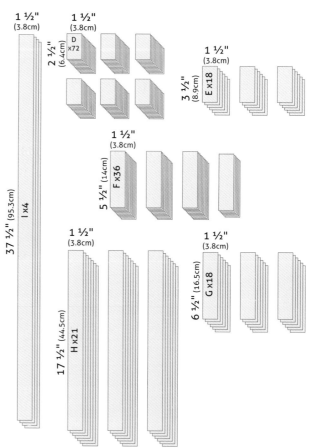

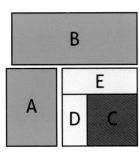

Figure A.

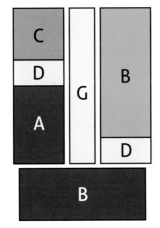

Figure B.

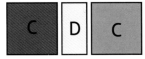

Figure C.

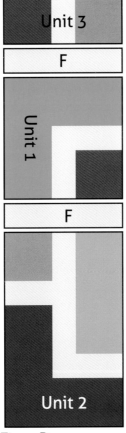

Figure D.

Piecing

Use a scant ¼" (6mm) seam allowance for all seams. Press seam allowances open or to the side as desired; mine are pressed open.

1. The quilt blocks are made from three units, sewn with sashing in between. Referring to Figure A, construct Unit 1 as follows.

    • Sew a C square to a D rectangle.

    • Then add an E rectangle (in the same color as D) on top.

    • Next, sew an A rectangle to the left.

    • And finally, sew a B rectangle (in the same color as A) to the top.

2. Construct Unit 2 as described below, following along with Figure B.

    • Sew a C square to a D rectangle.

    • Then add an A rectangle to the bottom. We'll call this one side. Set it aside for the time being.

    • Sew a B rectangle (shown in seafoam in the illustration) to a D rectangle, making another side.

    • Attach the two sides with a G rectangle in between.

    • Add a B rectangle (in the same color as A) to the bottom.

3. Construct Unit 3 by sewing a D rectangle between two C squares (Figure C).

4. Here comes the fun part, where you finish the column. Arrange the three units you've made however you like in a column, putting them in whatever order or placement that suits you, and then sew them with F rectangles in between (Figure D).

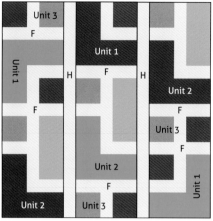
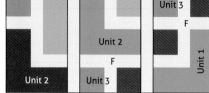

Figure E.

Figure F.

Figure G.

5. Repeat Steps 1–4 twice more to create three columns. Join the columns into a square block by sewing them together with H rectangles in between (Figure E). Repeat Steps 1–5 five more times to create six blocks total.

6. Create a row by joining two blocks together with an H strip between them, and attach an H strip on each end (Figure F). Repeat this twice more to create three rows.

7. Join all three rows together with the I strips between them and on each end (Figure G).

Finishing

Layer the backing, batting, and quilt top (page 50). Baste the layers and quilt as desired (page 48), then bind the raw edges (page 58).

QUILT IT!

This quilt has quite a lot going on with all its tiny pieces, so I kept the quilting basic with some crisscrossing diagonal lines. To make things super easy, I marked the lines with masking tape and used a walking foot. The resulting diamond pattern goes along with the "jewel" theme and also introduces just a bit of contrast to the whole piece.

Just My Size: Jeweled Lattice Baby Quilt

Instead of a baby quilt, would you like to make something bigger? Simply repeat more blocks to get the size that you need. Refer to the chart for the sizes and proper quantities, and create the quilt as described in the instructions.

Color variations: Would you like to make this quilt in a different color palette? Check out the options here to spark your creativity.

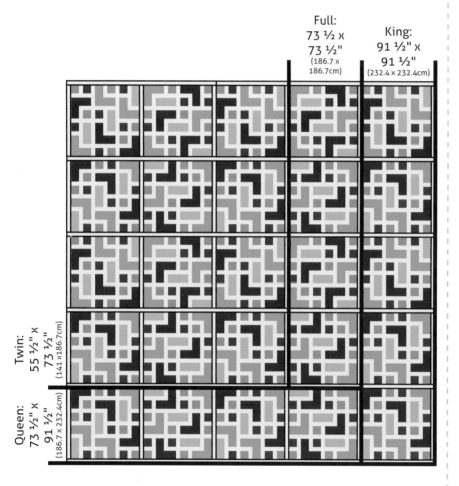

Full:
73 ½ x
73 ½"
(186.7 x
186.7cm)

King:
91 ½" x
91 ½"
(232.4 x 232.4cm)

Twin:
55 ½" x
73 ½"
(141 x186.7cm)

Queen:
73 ½" x
91 ½"
(186.7 x 232.4cm)

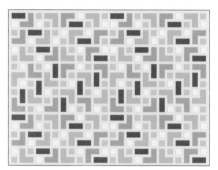

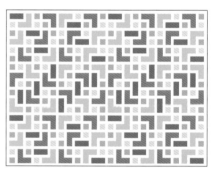

Quilt layout: Use the number of blocks indicated by the illustration and the chart to construct your quilt to size.

Quilting Simplified

96

Jeweled Lattice Baby Quilt

	Twin	Full	Queen	King
Finished size	55½" x 73½" (141 x 186.7cm)	73½" x 73½" (186.7 x 186.7cm)	73½" x 91½" (186.7 x 232.4cm)	91½" x 91½" (232.4 x 232.4cm)
Block configuration	3 blocks x 4 rows (12 total)	4 blocks x 4 rows (16 total)	4 blocks x 5 rows (20 total)	5 blocks x 5 rows (25 total)
Materials needed				
Violet and teal fabrics, each:	⅔ yd. (0.7m)	1 yd. (1m)	1¼ yd. (1.2m)	1⅓ yd. (1.3m)
Seafoam fabric	½ yd. (0.5m)	½ yd. (0.5m)	⅔ yd. (0.6m)	1 yd. (1m)
Orange and magenta fabrics, each:	½ yd. (0.5m)	½ yd. (0.5m)	⅔ yd. (0.6m)	¾ yd. (0.7m)
Border fabric	2½ yd. (2.3m)	3¼ yd. (3m)	4 yd. (3.7m)	5 yd. (4.6m)
Batting	64" x 82" (162.6 x 208.3cm)	82" x 82" (208.3 x 208.3cm)	82" x 100" (208.3 x 254cm)	100" x 100" (254 x 254cm)
Backing	2 yd. (1.9m) of 106" (269.2cm) wide backing	2½ yd. (2.3m) of 106" (269.2cm) wide backing	2½ yd. (2.3m) of 106" (269.2cm) wide backing	3 yd. (2.8m) of 106" (269.2cm) wide backing
Binding	⅔ yd. (0.7m)	¾ yd. (0.7m)	¾ yd. (0.7m)	1 yd. (1m)
Violet/Teal fabrics				
Strips to cut of each:	9 strips: 2½" (6.4cm) x width of fabric	12 strips: 2½" (6.4cm) x width of fabric	15 strips: 2½" (6.4cm) x width of fabric	18 strips: 2½" (6.4cm) x width of fabric
Subcut into:	36 rectangles: 3½" x 2½" (A) (8.9 x 6.4cm)	48 rectangles: 3½" x 2½" (A) (9 x 6.4cm)	60 rectangles: 3½" x 2½" (A) (9 x 6.4cm)	75 rectangles: 3½" x 2½" (A) (9 x 6.4cm)
	36 rectangles: 5½" x 2½" (B) (14 x 6.4cm)	48 rectangles: 5½" x 2½" (B) (14 x 6.4cm)	60 rectangles: 5½" x 2½" (B) (14 x 6.4cm)	75 rectangles: 5½" x 2½" (B) (14 x 6.4cm)
Seafoam fabric				
Strips to cut:	6 strips: 2½" (6.4cm) x width of fabric	7 strips: 2½" (6.4cm) x width of fabric	9 strips: 2½" (6.4cm) x width of fabric	11 strips: 2½" (6.4cm) x width of fabric
Subcut into:	36 rectangles: 5½" x 2½" (B) (14 x 6.4cm)	48 rectangles: 5½" x 2½" (B) (14 x 6.4cm)	60 rectangles: 5½" x 2½" (B) (14 x 6.4cm)	75 rectangles: 5½" x 2½" (B) (14 x 6.4cm)

Jeweled Lattice Baby Quilt Cutting Chart

	Twin	Full	Queen	King
Orange/magenta fabrics				
Strips to cut of each:	5 strips: 2½" (6.4cm) x width of fabric	6 strips: 2½" (6.4cm) x width of fabric	8 strips: 2½" (6.4cm) x width of fabric	10 strips: 2½" (6.4cm) x width of fabric
Subcut into:	72 squares: 2½" x 2½" (C) (6.4 x 6.4cm)	96 squares: 2½" x 2½" (C) (6.4 x 6.4cm)	120 squares: 2½" x 2½" (C) (6.4 x 6.4cm)	150 squares: 2½" x 2½" (C) (6.4 x 6.4cm)
Border fabric				
Strips to cut:	59 strips: 1½" (3.8cm) x width of fabric	74 strips: 1½" (3.8cm) x width of fabric	95 strips: 1½" (3.8cm) x width of fabric	114 strips: 1½" (3.8cm) x width of fabric
Horizontal sashing:	Chain 8 strips, then subcut into 5 strips: 55½" x 1½" (I) (139.7 x 3.8cm)	Chain 10 strips, then subcut into 5 strips: 73½" x 1½" (I) (186.7 x 3.8cm)	Chain 12 strips, then subcut into 6 strips: 73½" x 1½" (I) (186.7 x 3.8cm)	Chain 15 strips, then subcut into 6 strips: 91½" x 1½" (I) (232.4 x 3.8cm)
Working from the longest to the shortest to use the strips most efficiently, subcut into:	144 rectangles 2½" x 1½" (D) (6.4 x 3.8cm)	192 rectangles 2½" x 1½" (D) (6.4 x 3.8cm)	240 rectangles 2½" x 1½" (D) (6.4 x 3.8cm)	300 rectangles 2½" x 1½" (D) (6.4 x 3.8cm)
	36 rectangles 3½" x 1½" (E) (8.9 x 3.8cm)	48 rectangles 3½" x 1½" (E) (9 x 3.8cm)	60 rectangles 3½" x 1½" (E) (8.9 x 3.8cm)	75 rectangles 3½" x 1½" (E) (9 x 3.8cm)
	72 rectangles 5½" x 1½" (F) (14 x 3.8cm)	96 rectangles 5½" x 1½" (F) (14 x 3.8cm)	120 rectangles 5½" x 1½" (F) (14 x 3.8cm)	150 rectangles 5½" x 1½" (F) (14 x 3.8cm)
	36 rectangles 6½" x 1½" (G) (16.5 x 3.8cm)	48 rectangles 6½" x 1½" (G) (16.5 x 3.8cm)	60 rectangles 6½" x 1½" (G) (16.5 x 3.8cm)	75 rectangles 6½" x 1½" (G) (16.5 x 3.8cm)
	40 rectangles 17½" x 1½" (H) (44.5 x 3.8cm)	52 rectangles 17½" x 1½" (H) (44.5 x 3.8cm)	65 rectangles 17½" x 1½" (H) (44.5 x 3.8cm)	80 rectangles 17½" x 1½" (H) (44.5 x 3.8cm)

Artistic Arrows Quilt

Difficulty:

Techniques:
Rotary cutting (page 34)
Piecing (page 36)

Featured size: Twin (54½" x 78½"
[138.4 x 199.4cm]), see page 106 for
additional sizes

Suggested fabrics: Quilting cotton,
flannel, linen, poplin, voile, chambray

Tools
• Quilter's toolkit (see page 19)

Materials

Fabric	Yardage
Six coordinating focus fabrics	¾ yd. (0.7m) each
Batting	63" x 87" (160 x 221cm)
106" (269.2cm)-wide backing fabric	2 yd. (1.9m)
Binding fabric	⅔ yd. (0.7m)

This quilt is a real joy to put together. It's made entirely of strips in a completely randomized look that's pretty foolproof. The points at the end of every strip not only allow for some practice with triangles, but also give a fluid visual movement to the overall quilt, which looks slightly reminiscent of stained glass windows when done in a monochromatic color scheme.

PRECUT PERFECT!
A precut strip set can be used to make the twin-sized quilt here, but the strips must be at least 3½" (8.9cm) wide. Sets called dessert rolls are sometimes 5½" (14cm) wide and would work after trimming. Use the 2" (5.1cm) that's been trimmed to make the 2" x 2" (5.1 x 5.1cm) squares. The pack you choose needs at least 36 strips to make the twin quilt shown here. For the baby quilt you'll need 18 strips; for full, 60; for queen, 96; and for the king-size quilt, 108.

Cutting plan

Set aside all of the backing fabrics and batting to use later in the project; for now, gather all of the patchwork fabrics. Following the rotary cutting instructions on page 34, cut your fabric strips across the width of the fabric yardage. Make any subcuts as instructed, then sort and pile your fabrics according to letter, labeling them with a sticky note as necessary.

From the focus fabrics cut:

2 strips from each color: 2" (5.1cm) x width of fabric (12 total); subcut into:

- 24 squares from each color: 2" x 2" [5.1 x 5.1cm] (144 total); keep them separated by color.

6 strips from each color: 3½" (8.9cm) x width of fabric (36 total)

- Separate the strips into two stacks—Stack 1 and Stack 2—of random colors containing 18 strips each.

- Subcut each strip in Stack 1 into two pieces, about 8" (20cm) and 32" (80cm). Accuracy isn't crucial here; just make all 18 pieces in each of these resulting stacks have the same length.

- Subcut each strip in Stack 2 into two pieces as well, about 13" (35cm) and 27" (70cm).

- Place each stack into its own bag and label them A through D.

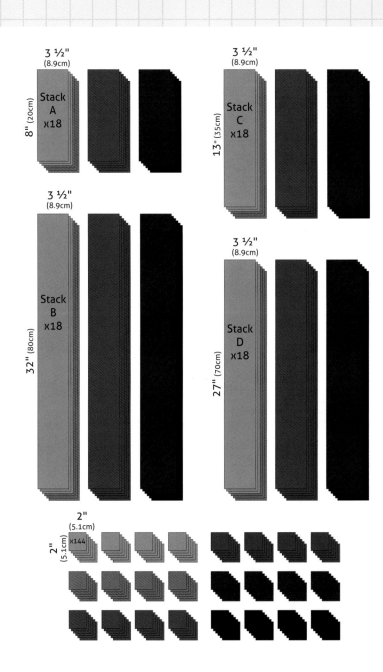

Figure A.

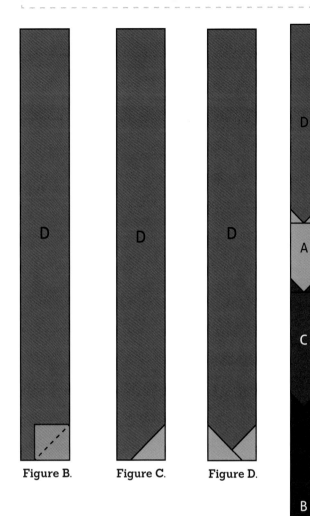

Figure B.　**Figure C.**　**Figure D.**

Figure E.

Piecing

Use a scant ¼" (6mm) seam allowance for all seams. Press seam allowances open or to the side as desired; mine are pressed open.

The randomness of the quilt is achieved by taking a random strip from each bag to construct the columns for the quilt. Make sure only one strip from each bag is taken for every column to ensure each column is the same length.

1. To begin the first column, grab a strip from each bag in a random order, such as D, A, C, B. The D strip will be the first in the column, A the second. Now find two 2½" (6.4cm) squares that match the second color (A) (Figure A).

2. Align the first square with the bottom right corner of the D strip with right sides facing. Draw a line going diagonally through the square from the upper outside corner to the lower inside corner (Figure B).

3. Sew along the line you drew, and then trim away the excess fabric. Press (Figure C).

4. Align the second square with the bottom left corner of the D strip opposite the first square. As you did in Steps 3 and 4, draw a diagonal line, sew the square, and then trim and press. Your strip now has triangle corners at one end (Figure D).

5. Now you'll add more strips to form a column. Sew the A strip to the end of the D strip with triangle corners. Repeat Steps 2–6 with the A strip, adding C-colored squares to the bottom. Once you've done that, sew the C strip to the end of the A strip with triangle ends, adding B-colored squares to the bottom. Finally, sew the B strip to the end of the C strip with triangle ends (Figure E). Note that the last strip needs no squares.

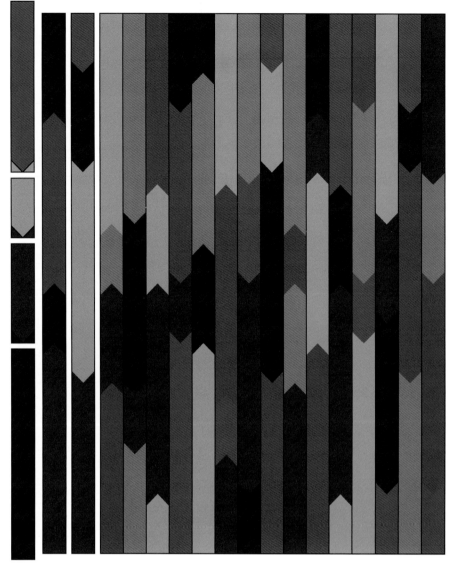

Figure F.

6. Repeat Steps 1–5 seventeen more times to create eighteen total columns for the quilt. Be sure to keep your strip arrangement (C, D, B, A, etc.) random every time.

7. Arrange all your strips together in a way that's pleasing to you, flipping them occasionally if you wish, so you can achieve the randomness you prefer (Figure F).

8. When your columns are arranged as you like, sew them all together along the long edges. It helps to pin them from the center outward to be sure that they line up perfectly all through their length.

Finishing

Layer the backing, batting, and quilt top (page 50), baste the layers, quilt as desired (page 48), and bind the raw edges (page 58).

QUILT IT!

When finished, this quilt reminded me of a stained glass window, so I used repetitive quilting to reinforce the gentle, calm beauty that I think of when I see stained glass. I used my walking foot to give the columns outline quilting. For a little added pop, I used masking tape to run a line parallel to one arrow point in the bottom right and top left corners and quilted along those guides for a few sharp angles.

Just My Size: Artistic Arrows Quilt

Would you like to make this quilt in just the size you need? To do so, you'll need to create different combinations of stacks and strips to achieve different lengths. The math is all worked out for you in the chart here. Simply follow the instructions as before, but be aware you'll be using lots more assorted bags. Note that the stacks are paired off to indicate how each stack of 40" (101.5cm) strips gets cut in half to form a pair of differently sized strips than in the original cutting plan on page 102.

Color variations: Would you like to make this quilt in a different color palette? Check out the options here to spark your creativity.

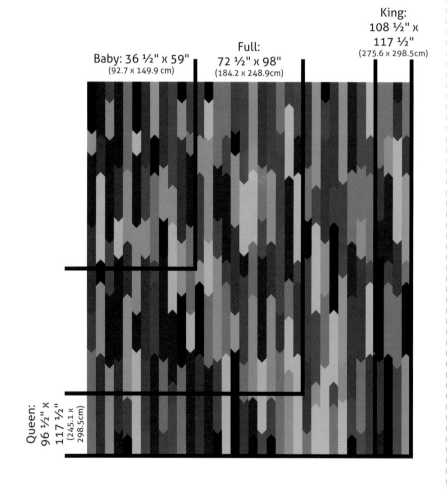

King:
108 ½" x
117 ½"
(275.6 x 298.5cm)

Full:
72 ½" x 98"
(184.2 x 248.9cm)

Baby: 36 ½" x 59"
(92.7 x 149.9 cm)

Queen:
96 ½" x
117 ½"
(245.1 x
298.5cm)

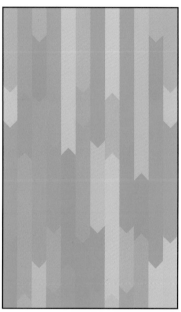

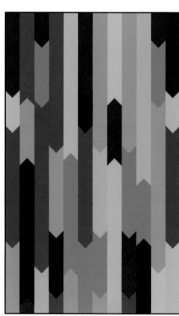

Quilt layout: Use the number of strips and columns indicated by the illustration and the chart to construct your quilt to the desired size.

Artistic Arrows Quilt

	Baby	Full	Queen	King
Finished size	36½" x 59" (92.7 x 149.9cm)	72½" x 98" (184.2 x 248.9cm)	96½" x 117½" (245.1 x 298.5cm)	108½" x 117½" (275.6 x 298.5cm)
Block configuration	12 columns x 3 strips	24 columns x 5 strips	32 columns x 6 strips	36 columns x 6 strips
Materials needed				
Coordinating focus fabrics:	½ yd. (0.5m) each of 6 fabrics	1¼ yd. (1.2m) each of 6 fabrics	1½ yd. (1.4m) each of 8 fabrics	1½ yd. (1.4m) each of 9 fabrics
Batting	45" x 67" (114.3 x 170.2cm)	81" x 106" (205.7 x 269.2cm)	105" x 126" (266.7 x 320cm)	117" x 126" (297.2 x 320cm)
Backing	2 yd. (1.9m) of 60" (152.4cm) wide backing	4¾ yd. (4.5m) of 60" (152.4cm) wide backing	3⅔ yd. (3.4m) of 106" (269.2cm) wide backing	3⅔ yd. (3.4m) of 118" (299.7cm) wide backing
Binding	½ yd. (0.5m)	¾ yd. (0.7m)	1 yd. (1m)	1 yd. (1m)
Strips to cut from each color:	1 strip (6 total) 2" (5.1cm) x width of fabric	2 strips (12 total) 2" (5.1cm) x width of fabric	3 strips (24 total) 2" (5.1cm) x width of fabric	3 strips (27 total) 2" (5.1cm) x width of fabric
Subcut into:	12 squares: (72 total) 2" x 2" (5.1 x 5.1cm)	40 squares: (240 total) 2" x 2" (5.1 x 5.1cm)	48 squares: (384 total) 2" x 2" (5.1 x 5.1cm)	48 squares: (432 total) 2" x 2" (5.1 x 5.1cm)
Strips to cut from each color:	3 strips (18 total) 3½" (8.9cm) x width of fabric	10 strips (60 total) 3½" (8.9cm) x width of fabric	12 strips (96 total) 3½" (8.9cm) x width of fabric	12 strips (108 total) 3½" (8.9cm) x width of fabric
Using the material as efficiently as possible, subcut into:	12 strips: (Bag A) 3½" x 20" (8.9 x 50.8cm)	24 strips: (Bag A) 3½" x 20" (8.9 x 50.8cm)	32 strips: (Bag A) 3½" x 7" (8.9 x 17.8cm)	36 strips: (Bag A) 3½" x 7" (8.9 x 17.8cm)
	12 strips: (Bag B) 3½" x 12" (8.9 x 30.5cm)	24 strips: (Bag B) 3½" x 12" (8.9 x 30.5cm)	32 strips: (Bag B) 3½" x 33" (8.9 x 83.8cm)	36 strips: (Bag B) 3½" x 33" (8.9 x 83.8cm)
	12 strips: (Bag C) 3½" x 28" (8.9 x 71.1cm)	24 strips: (Bag C) 3½" x 28" (8.9 x 71.1cm)	32 strips: (Bag C) 3½" x 12" (8.9 x 30.5cm)	36 strips: (Bag C) 3½" x 12" (8.9 x 30.5cm)
		24 strips: (Bag D) 3½" x 7" (8.9 x 17.8cm)	32 strips: (Bag D) 3½" x 28" (8.9 x 71.1cm)	36 strips: (Bag D) 3½" x 28" (8.9 x 71.1cm)
		24 strips: (Bag E) 3½" x 33" (8.9 x 83.8cm)	32 strips: (Bag E) 3½" x 17" (8.9 x 43.2cm)	36 strips: (Bag E) 3½" x 17" (8.9 x 43.2cm)
			32 strips: (Bag F) 3½" x 23" (8.9 x 58.4cm)	36 strips: (Bag F) 3½" x 23" (8.9 x 58.4cm)

Ombré Trapezoid Quilt

Difficulty:

Techniques:
Rotary cutting (page 34)
Piecing (page 36)
Making templates (page 76)

Featured size: Full (71¾" x 88½"
[182.2 x 224.8cm]), see page 114 for
additional sizes

Suggested fabrics: Quilting cotton,
flannel, linen, poplin, voile, chambray

Tools
- Quilter's toolkit (see page 19)
- Template-making material (see Mini
  Lesson: Making Templates, page 76)

Materials

Fabric	Yardage
Various coordinating focus fabrics	3¼ yd. (3m) total
Background fabric	5⅔ yd. (5.2m)
Batting	80" x 96" (203.2 x 243.8cm)
106" (269.2cm)-wide backing fabric	2⅓ yd. (2.2m)
Binding fabric	¾ yd. (0.7m)

What's so amazing about quilts—especially modern ones—is how a simple shape like a trapezoid, when repeated over the whole expanse of your quilt, can turn into a fresh and vibrant design. That idea comes to life here in this quilt, which has a funky, almost mod, look to it. The gradated colors blending from magenta to blue add an extra twist.

PRECUT PERFECT!
The trapezoid template for this project fits perfectly onto 10" (25.4cm) charm pack squares. Simply purchase a pack that has at least as many squares as there are trapezoids in your quilt; for the full-size one shown here, that's 72. Then trace the shape onto one of your charm squares and you're good to go. And you can use any excess to piece the back of your quilt.

Cutting plan

Following the instructions for Making Templates on page 76, make a template of the pattern on page 111. Set aside until needed. Set aside all of the backing fabrics and batting for later use; gather all of the patchwork fabrics for now. Following the rotary cutting instructions on page 34, cut your fabric strips down the width of the fabric yardage. Make any subcuts as instructed, then sort and pile your fabrics according to letter, labeling with a sticky note as necessary.

From the focus fabrics cut:

12 strips: 9½" (24.1cm) x width of fabric; subcut into:

- 72 rectangles: 6½" x 9½" [16.5 x 24.1cm] (A)

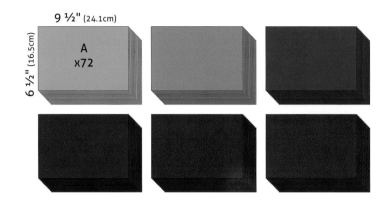

From the background fabric cut:

36 strips: 3" (7.6cm) x width of fabric; subcut into:

- 144 rectangles: 10" x 3" [25.4 x 7.6cm] (B)

5 strips: 6½" (16.5cm) x width of fabric; subcut into:

- 71 rectangles: 2½" x 6½" [6.4 x 16.5cm] (C)

5 strips: 11½" (29.2cm) x width of fabric; subcut into:

- 72 rectangles: 2½" x 11½" [6.4 x 29.2cm] (D)

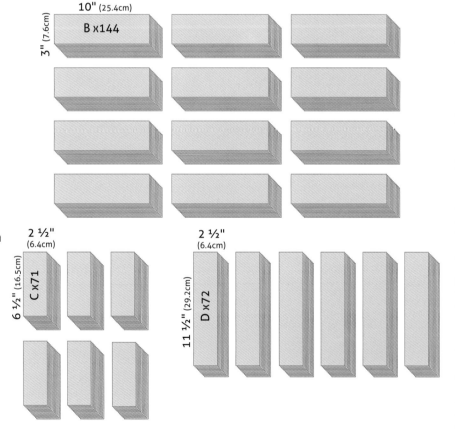

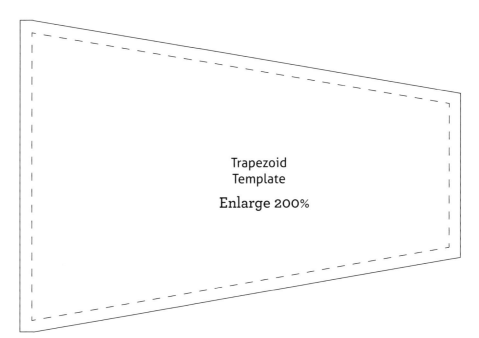

Trapezoid
Template

Enlarge 200%

Piecing

Use a scant ¼" (6mm) seam allowance for all seams. Press seam allowances open or to the side as desired; mine are pressed open.

1. To create the trapezoid shapes, trace and cut the template above from template plastic. Use the template you cut from template plastic to mark and trim all 72 rectangles cut from the focus fabrics (Figure A).

2. Align one long edge of a B rectangle with one slanted edge of a trapezoid with right sides facing as shown in Figure B. Then sew the pieces together. Repeat on the other slanted edge of the trapezoid with another rectangle.

3. Trim the rectangle to 9½" x 6½" [24.1 x 16.5cm] (Figure C).

4. Sew a C rectangle to the wide end of the trapezoid shape, and sew a D rectangle to one side of the trapezoid shape (Figure D). Repeat Steps 1–4 seventy-one more times to make seventy-two trapezoid blocks.

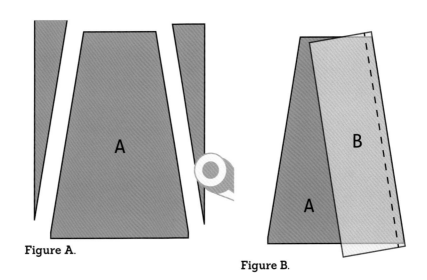

A

Figure A.

B

A

Figure B.

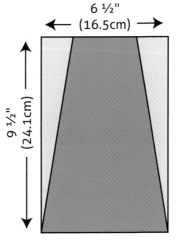

6 ½"
(16.5cm)

9 ½"
(24.1cm)

Figure C.

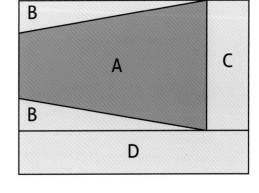

B

A

C

B

D

Figure D.

Figure E.

Odd row

Unit 1

Figure F.

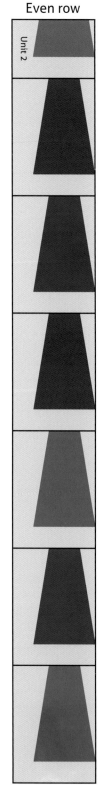

Even row

Unit 2

Figure G.

5. Gather 11 of your trapezoid blocks and cut them exactly in half widthwise in order to create the end blocks. Label the stack of the ones containing the narrow ends of the trapezoids Unit 1, and the ones with the wide ends Unit 2 (Figure E).

6. For the full-sized quilt shown here, create an odd row of 6 blocks plus one Unit 1 block at the end. Repeat this 5 more times to make a total of 6 odd rows (Figure F).

7. Create an even row of 6 blocks as you did in the previous step, but add a Unit 2 block at the beginning. Repeat this 4 more times to make a total of 5 even rows (Figure G).

8. Sew together alternating odd and even rows to create the quilt top.

Finishing
Layer the backing, batting, and quilt top (page 50), baste the layers, quilt as desired (page 48), and bind the raw edges (page 58).

QUILT IT!
The retro look of this quilt made me want to use a similar style in my free-motion quilting. I used geometric stippling, sometimes called maze or circuit board quilting. It is much like regular stippling (see page 54), but only uses horizontal and vertical lines. The occasional loops give the quilting the look of a circuit board, which feels a bit retro to me.

Just My Size: **Ombré Trapezoid Quilt**

Would you like to make this quilt in just the size you need? Simply repeat the trapezoid block with half blocks at the end and beginning of the rows as the chart and illustration show. Refer to the block and material requirements here to get started, then assemble the rest of the quilt as in the instructions.

Color variations: Would you like to make this quilt in a different color palette? Check out the options here to spark your creativity.

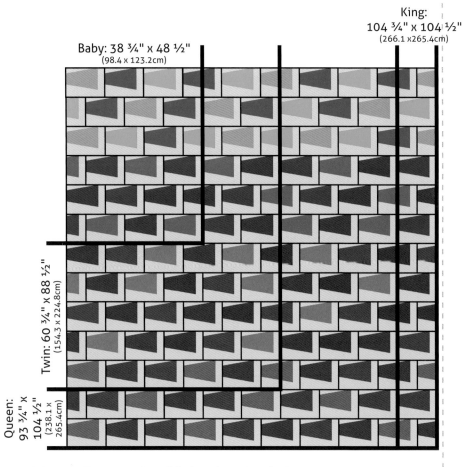

Baby: 38 ¾" x 48 ½"
(98.4 x 123.2cm)

King:
104 ¾" x 104 ½"
(266.1 x265.4cm)

Twin: 60 ¾" x 88 ½"
(154.3 x 224.8cm)

Queen:
93 ¾" x
104 ½"
(238.1 x
265.4cm)

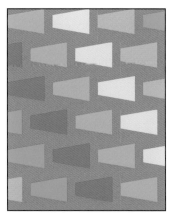

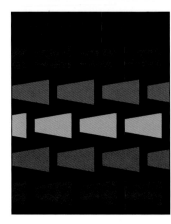

Quilt layout: Use the number of blocks indicated by the illustration and the chart to construct your quilt to size.

Ombré Trapezoid Quilt

	Baby	Twin	Queen	King
Finished size	38¾" x 48½" (98.4 x 123.2cm)	60¾" x 88½" (154.3 x 224.8cm)	93¾" x 104½" (238.1 x 265.4cm)	104¾" x 104½" (266.1 x 265.4cm)
Block configuration	3.5 blocks x 6 rows (21 blocks)	5.5 blocks x 11 rows (61 total)	8.5 blocks x 13 rows (111 total)	9.5 blocks x 13 rows (124 total)
Materials needed				
Various coordinating focus fabrics, totaling:	1¼ yd. (1.2m)	3 yd. (2.8m)	5¼ yd. (4.9m)	5⅔ yd. (5.2m)
Background fabrics	2 yd. (1.9m)	4⅔ yd. (4.3m)	8¼ yd. (7.6m)	9¼ yd. (8.5m)
Batting	47" x 57" (119.4 x 144.8cm)	69" x 97" (175.2 x 246.4cm)	102" x 113" (259.1 x 287cm)	113" x 113" (287 x 287cm)
Backing	1½ yd. (1.4m) of 60" (152.4cm) wide backing	2 yd. (1.9m) of 106" (269.2cm) wide backing	3 yd. (2.8m) of 118" (299.7cm) wide backing	3¼ yd. (3m) of 118" (299.7cm) wide backing
Binding	½ yd. (0.5m)	¾ yd. (0.7m)	1 yd. (1m)	1 yd. (1m)
Various focus fabrics				
Strips to cut:	4 strips: 9½" (24.1cm) x width of fabric	11 strips: 9½" (24.1cm) x width of fabric	19 strips: 9½" (24.1cm) x width of fabric	21 strips: 9½" (24.1cm) x width of fabric
Subcut into:	21 rectangles: 6½" x 9½" (A) (16.5 x 24.1cm)	61 rectangles: 6½" x 9½" (A) (16.5 x 24.1cm)	111 rectangles: 6½" x 9½" (A) (16.5 x 24.1cm)	124 rectangles: 6½" x 9½" (A) (16.5 x 24.1cm)
Background fabric				
Strips to cut:	11 strips: 3" (7.6cm) x width of fabric	31 strips: 3" (7.6cm) x width of fabric	56 strips: 3" (7.6cm) x width of fabric	62 strips: 3" (7.6cm) x width of fabric
Subcut into:	42 rectangles: 10" x 3" (B) (25.4 x 7.6cm)	122 rectangles: 10" x 3" (B) (25.4 x 7.6cm)	222 rectangles: 10" x 3" (B) (25.4 x 7.6cm)	248 rectangles: 10" x 3" (B) (25.4 x 7.6cm)
Strips to cut:	2 strips: 6½" (16.5cm) x width of fabric	4 strips: 6½" (16.5cm) x width of fabric	7 strips: 6½" (16.5cm) x width of fabric	8 strips: 6½" (16.5cm) x width of fabric
Subcut into:	21 rectangles: 2½" x 6½" (C) (6.4 x 16.5cm)	61 rectangles: 2½" x 6½" (C) (6.4 x 16.5cm)	111 rectangles: 2½" x 6½" (C) (6.4 x 16.5cm)	124 rectangles: 2½" x 6½" (C) (6.4 x 16.5cm)
Strips to cut:	2 strips: 11½" (29.2cm) x width of fabric	4 strips: 11½" (29.2cm) x width of fabric	7 strips: 11½" (29.2cm) x width of fabric	8 strips: 11½" (29.2cm) x width of fabric
Subcut into:	21 rectangles: 2½" x 11½" (D) (6.4 x 29.2cm)	61 rectangles: 2½" x 11½" (D) (6.4 x 29.2cm)	111 rectangles: 2½" x 11½" (D) (6.4 x 29.2cm)	124 rectangles: 2½" x 11½" (D) (6.4 x 29.2cm)

Mod Log Cabin Quilt

Difficulty:

Techniques:
Rotary cutting (page 34)
Piecing (page 36)
Log cabin blocks

Featured size: Queen (84½" x 110" [214.6 x 279.4cm]), see page 123 for additional sizes

Suggested fabrics: Quilting cotton, flannel, linen, poplin, voile, chambray

Tools
- Quilter's toolkit (see page 19)

Materials

Fabric	Yardage
6 coordinating focus fabrics	¾ yd. (0.7m) each
Background fabric	6½ yd. (6m)
Batting	92½" x 118" (235 x 299.7cm)
106" (269.2cm)-wide backing fabric	3½ yd. (3.2m)
Binding fabric	1 yd. (1m)

This quilt will have you take a dip into improvisational quilting, one of the many useful techniques used in modern quilting. If meticulous measuring and cutting doesn't appeal to you, then this method might have you hooked. The log cabin blocks in this quilt will give you lots of room for interpretation, so be prepared to experiment!

PRECUT PERFECT!
A precut strip set can be used for the focus fabrics in the queen-sized quilt shown here, but they must be at least 4" (10.2cm) wide. Sets called dessert rolls are sometimes 5½" (14cm) wide and would give you lots of fabric for improvisation. The pack you choose needs to contain at least 60 strips to cover the focus fabrics for the queen-size quilt shown here. For the baby quilt, you'll need at least 18; for twin, 40; for full, 50; and for king, 70.

Cutting plan

Set aside all of the backing fabrics and batting; for now, gather all of the patchwork fabrics. Following the rotary cutting instructions on page 34, cut your fabric strips down the width of the fabric yardage. Make any subcuts as instructed, then sort and pile your fabrics according to letter, labeling with a sticky note as necessary.

From the focus fabrics cut:

2 strips from each color: 2½" x 40" [6.4 x 101.6cm] (12 total) (A)

1 strip from each color: 1½" x 40" (3.8 x 101.6cm) (accent strip for the improvisational log cabin blocks)*

2 strips from each color: 2" x 40" (5.1 x 101.6cm) (accent strips for the improvisational log cabin blocks)*

2 strips from each color: 2" x 40" (5.1 x 101.6cm) (block strips for the improvisational log cabin blocks)*

3 strips from each color: 3" x 40" (7.6 x 101.6cm) (block strips for the improvisational log cabin blocks)*

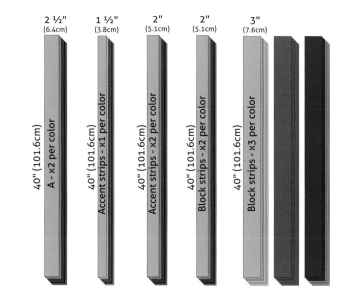

From the background fabric cut:

24 strips: 6½" x 40" [16.5 x 101.6cm] (B)

2 strips: 4" x 40" (10.2 x 101.6cm) (center squares for the improvisational log cabin blocks)*

2 strips: 6" x 40" (15.2 x 101.6cm) (center squares for the improvisational log cabin blocks)*

9 strips: 3" x 40" (7.6 x 101.6cm) (block sides for the improvisational log cabin blocks)*

5 strips: 6" x 40" (15.2 x 101.6cm) (block sides for the improvisational log cabin blocks)*

*Note: If you're feeling daring, leave these uncut for now and decide your own sizes in the log cabin blocks section on page 120.

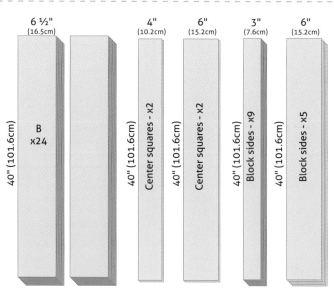

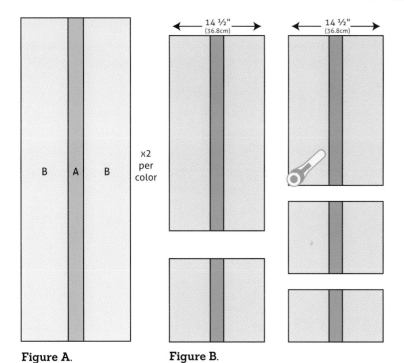

x2 per color

Figure A.

Figure B.

14 ½"
(36.8cm)

14 ½"
(36.8cm)

Piecing

Use a scant ¼" (6mm) seam allowance for all seams. Press seam allowances open or to the side as desired; mine are pressed open.

The strip sets

1. Sew a 6½" (16.5cm)-wide B background strip to each side of a 2½" (6.4cm)-wide A focus fabric strip, creating a strip set with a center stripe (Figure A). Repeat this with the other A strip of the same color so you have a pair of strip sets. Repeat with the remaining 6½" (16.5cm)-wide B background strips and 2½" (6.4cm)-wide A focus strips. When finished, you will have 12 strip sets sewn together, 2 in each color of your focus fabric collection.

2. As shown in Figure B, subcut one pair of strip sets into five rectangles, varying the lengths to make a random combination, such as (23" + 17") [58.4 + 43.2cm] and (20" + 12" + 8") [50.8 + 30.5 + 20.3]. Repeat this with the strip sets from the rest of your colors, striving to make each rectangle a different length.

LOG CABIN BLOCKS

Log cabin blocks are a very traditional kind of block that has been around for generations; they're made from a center square with strips added to the sides in an indefinite number, making the block bigger and bigger as you sew. There are a few variations of adding the strips, such as Courthouse Steps or going completely improvised. With carefully chosen fabric colors, you can create some gorgeous variations!

Log cabin blocks. This very traditional block can be modified in lots of modern ways, either by making color variations or by varying the shape of the logs.

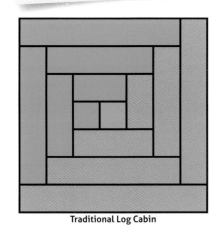

Traditional Log Cabin

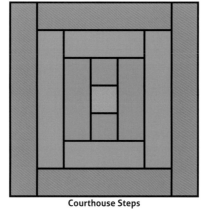

Courthouse Steps

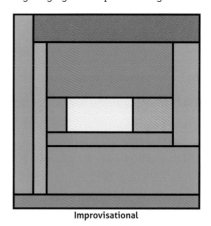

Improvisational

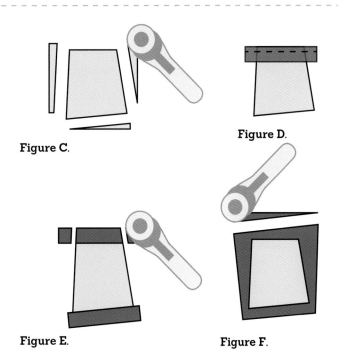

Figure C.

Figure D.

Figure E.

Figure F.

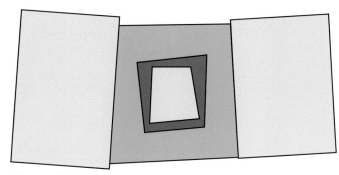

Figure G.

The log cabin blocks

For each color in your focus fabric collection you will need 4 log cabin blocks, pieced in an askew, improvisational style here. The measurements listed in the assembly steps are optional, but the trimmed finished sizes of the blocks should be the same. The finished sizes of the blocks should be:

- 12" x 14½" (30.5 x 36.8cm)
- 11" x 14½" (27.9 x 36.8cm)
- 6" x 14½" (15.2 x 36.8cm)
- 5" x 14½" (12.7 x 36.8cm)

1. Start creating your smallest, wonky 5" (12.7cm) log cabin by trimming a 4" x 4" (10.2 x 10.2cm) square from a 4" (10.2cm)-wide B center square strip. Trim off the edges of the block until it makes an uneven square that's to your liking (Figure C).

2. Cut a piece of fabric from your narrowest A focus fabric accent strip so that it's wider than the top edge of your center square. Sew it along the top edge of your wonky square with right sides facing (Figure D).

3. Press the fabric open, then trim the excess accent fabric from the top edge by lining up your ruler against the sides of the center square. Repeat Steps 2 and 3 for the bottom of the square as well (Figure E).

4. Add accent strips to the sides of the block by repeating Steps 2 and 3 so the accent fabric completely encloses the center square. When trimming, feel free to make the edges wonky just like for the center square in Step 1 (Figure F).

5. For the final round of the log cabin, select a coordinating color from your A focus fabric block strips. Using the narrowest strip, repeat Steps 2–4 to create the outer square. Before going on to the next step, make sure your block is at least 5" (12.7cm) tall. If it's not, add more strips of focus fabric to the bottom and top.

6. To achieve the effect we're going for in this quilt, each log cabin block needs two background strips on the sides. Cut the pieces from the widest of your B background block side strips and sew them to each side of your log cabin (Figure G).

14 ½"
(36.8cm)

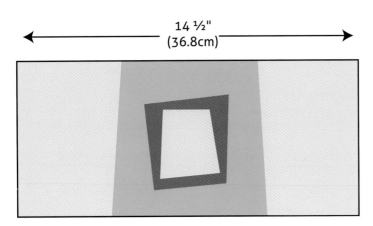

Figure H.

7. As shown in Figure H, trim your block to 14½" x 5" (36.8 x 12.7cm). Using the same color scheme, create three other blocks in the other sizes listed. To do this, repeat Steps 1–6 with your remaining improv strips. Use the narrower B center square, A accent, and A block strips for the smaller blocks and the wider ones for the large blocks. Conversely, use the wider B block side strips for the small blocks and the narrower strips for the large blocks.

8. Repeat Steps 1–7 for the rest of the colors in your focus fabric collection. When finished, you will have 6 sets of 4 blocks. Make a pile of blocks and strip set rectangles you created earlier for each color.

9. Now you'll sew the columns. Each one is made by sewing together the log cabin blocks and strip sets from one color. Sew them in a column, alternating the log cabins with the strip sets, choosing a random selection each time. Your finished column should have a strip set on each end (Figure I). Create a column for each of the rest of your colors, placing the rectangles in a different order each time to achieve randomness.

10. Join the finished columns to complete the quilt top.

Finishing
Layer the backing, batting, and quilt top (page 50), baste the layers, quilt as desired (page 48), and bind the raw edges (page 58).

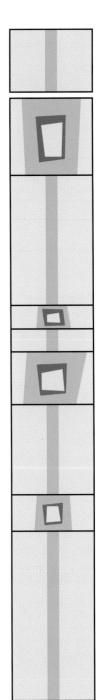

Figure I.

QUILT IT!
While searching for a mod-inspired motif to quilt this piece, I stumbled across some amazing and approachable ideas in Japanese sashiko embroidery. I modified a pattern called *kasumi*, or mist, to quilt this project. The design looks like floating waves and is very adaptable. I thought the curves offset the sharp angles in the log cabin blocks just enough, while still going with the theme of the quilt.

Just My Size: **Mod Log Cabin Quilt**

Would you like to make this quilt in a different size? To accommodate different sizes, you'll need to create strip sets of different lengths and different sizes of improv log cabin blocks, although the construction is still the same. See the chart and illustration to get the correct materials and block sizes, and then follow the instructions as before.

Color variations: Would you like to make this quilt in a different color palette? Check out the options here to spark your creativity.

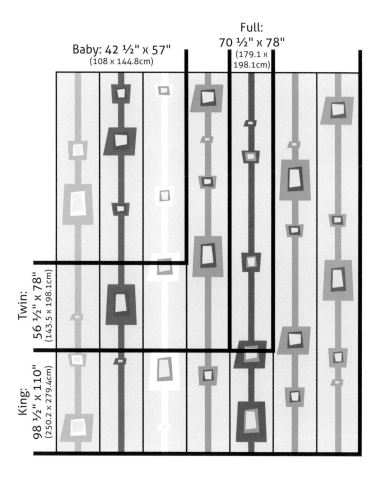

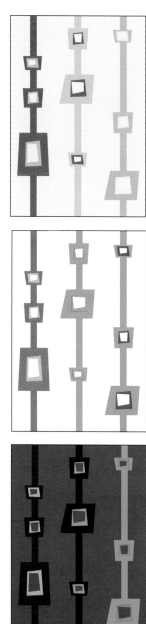

Quilt layout: Use the number of blocks indicated by the illustration and the chart to construct your quilt to size.

Mod Log Cabin Quilt

	Baby	Twin	Full	King
Finished size	42½" x 57" (108 x 144.8cm)	56½" x 78" (143.5 x 198.1cm)	70½" x 78" (179.1 x 198.1cm)	98½" x 110" (250.2 x 279.4cm)
Block configuration	3 blocks x 3 rows (9 blocks)	4 blocks x 4 rows (16 total)	4 blocks x 5 rows (20 total)	4 blocks x 7 rows (35 total)
Block sizes for each color:	14½" x (4", 7", 9") (36.8 x [10.2, 17.8, 22.9cm])	14½" x (6", 9", 12", 15") (36.8 x [15.2, 22.9, 30.5, 38.1cm])	14½" x (6", 9", 12", 15") (36.8 x [15.2, 22.9, 30.5, 38.1cm])	14½" x (5", 6", 11", 12") (36.8 x [12.7, 15.2, 27.9, 30.5cm])
Materials needed				
Coordinating focus fabrics	½ yd. (0.5m) each of 3 fabrics	1 yd. (1m) each of 4 fabrics	1 yd. (1m) each of 5 fabrics	¾ yd. (0.7m) each of 7 fabrics
Background fabrics	2¼ yd. (2.1m)	3⅓ yd. (3.1m)	4 yd. (3.7m)	7⅔ yd. (7m)
Batting	51" x 65" (129.5 x 165.1cm)	65" x 86" (165.1 x 218.4cm)	79" x 86" (200.7 x 218.4cm)	107" x 118" (271.8 x 299.7cm)
Backing	2 yd. (1.9m) of 60" (152.4cm) wide backing	2 yd. (1.9m) of 106" (269.2cm) wide backing	2¼ yd. (2.1m) of 106" (269.2cm) wide backing	3½ yd. (3.2m) of 118" (299.7cm) wide backing
Binding	½ yd. (0.5m)	⅔ yd. (0.7m)	⅔ yd. (0.7m)	1 yd. (1m)
Focus fabrics				
For strip sets; cut from each color:	1 strip: 2½" (6.4cm) x width of fabric (A)	1 strip: 2½" (6.4cm) x width of fabric (A)	1 strip: 2½" (6.4cm) x width of fabric (A)	2 strips: 2½" (6.4cm) x width of fabric (A)
Improv fabric; cut from each color:	Accents; 2 strips: 2" (5.1cm) x width of fabric	Accents; 2 strips of each: 1½" (3.8cm), 2½" (6.4cm), all x width of fabric	Accents; 2 strips: 1½" (3.8cm), 2 strips: 2½" (6.4cm), all x width of fabric	Accents; 1 strip: 1½" (3.8cm), 2 strips: 2" (5.1cm), all x width of fabric
	Block strips; 1 strip of each: 2½" (6.4cm), 3" (7.6cm), 5" (12.7cm), all x width of fabric	Block strips; 2 strips: 3" (7.6cm), 3 strips: 4" (10.2cm), all x width of fabric	Block strips; 2 strips: 3" (7.6cm), 3 strips: 4" (10.2cm), all x width of fabric	Block strips; 2 strips: 2" (5.1cm), 3 strips: 3" (7.6cm), all x width of fabric

Mod Log Cabin Quilt

	Baby	Twin	Full	King
Background fabrics				
For strip sets; cut:	6 strips: 6½" (16.5cm) x width of fabric (B)	8 strips: 6½" (16.5cm) x width of fabric (B)	10 strips: 6½" (16.5cm) x width of fabric (B)	28 strips: 6½" (16.5cm) x width of fabric (B)
Improv fabric:	Center squares; 1 strip of each: 3" (7.6cm), 4" (10.2cm), 5" (12.7cm), all x width of fabric	Center squares; 1 strip of each: 4" (10.2cm), 5" (12.7cm), 7" (17.8cm), 8" (20.4cm), all x width of fabric	Center squares; 1 strip of each: 4" (10.2cm), 5" (12.7cm), 7" (17.8cm), 8" (20.4cm), all x width of fabric	Center squares; 2 strips: 4" (10.2cm), 3 strips: 6" (15.2cm), all x width of fabric
	Block sides; 2 strips: 4" (10.2cm), 2 strips: 5" (12.7cm), 1 strip: 6" (15.2cm), all x width of fabric	Block sides; 7 strips: 3" (7.6cm), 4 strips: 5" (12.7cm), all x width of fabric	Block sides; 8 strips: 3" (7.6cm), 5 strips: 5" (12.7cm), all x width of fabric	Block sides; 10 strips: 3" (7.6cm), 6 strips: 6" (15.2cm), all x width of fabric
Strip sets				
Subcut into:	4 rectangles for each color	5 rectangles for each color	5 rectangles for each color	5 rectangles for each color

Ripple Quilt

Difficulty:

Techniques:
Rotary cutting (page 34)
Piecing (page 36)
Log cabin blocks

Featured size: Full (70½" x 88½" [179.1 x 224.8cm]), see page 133 for additional sizes

Suggested fabrics: Quilting cotton, flannel, linen, poplin, voile, chambray

Tools
• Quilter's toolkit (see page 19)

Materials

Fabric	Yardage
5 coordinating focus fabrics	⅔ yd. (0.7m)
5 background fabrics	½ yd. (0.5m)
Sashing fabric	⅔ yd. (0.7m)
Batting	79" x 97" (200.6 x 246.4cm)
106" (269.2cm)-wide backing fabric	2¼ yd. (2.1m)
Binding fabric	¾ yd. (0.7m)

While the design for this quilt looks a little op art, it's actually inspired by ripples of water from pebbles dropped in a pond. When the quilt is made with highly contrasting fabrics, the concentric squares are sure to make your eyes dance. However, when done in a variety of matching fabrics, it takes on a softer, more Zen-like appearance. The blocks here are much bigger than anything we've worked with elsewhere in the book, so it's a bit of a challenge, but well worth the extra effort!

PRECUT PERFECT!
A jelly roll set of 2½" (6.4cm) strips can be used to replace both the focus fabrics and the background fabrics for this quilt. The result will look much scrappier, but still maintain the ripple effect. For this full-sized quilt, buy a pack of at least 45 strips for the focus fabrics and 43 strips for the background and sashing fabrics. For a baby quilt you'll need at least 18 focus strips and 16 background strips; for twin, 36 and 34; for queen size, 72 and 67; and for king, 81 and 77.

Cutting plan

Set aside all of the backing fabrics and batting for later in the project; gather all of the patchwork fabrics for now. Following the rotary cutting instructions on page 34, cut your fabric strips across the width of the fabric yardage. Make any subcuts as instructed, then sort and pile your fabrics according to letter, labeling them with a sticky note as necessary.

From the focus fabrics cut:

9 strips from each color: 2½" (6.4cm) x width of fabric (45 total); for each color, subcut as follows, cutting the longer rectangles first, then cutting the shorter rectangles from the remaining fabric:

- 1 square, 2½" x 2½" [6.4 x 6.4cm] (A)
- 2 rectangles, 6½" x 2½" [16.5 x 6.4cm] (B)
- 2 rectangles, 10½" x 2½" [26.7 x 6.4cm] (C)
- 2 rectangles, 14½" x 2½" [36.8 x 6.4cm] (D)
- 2 rectangles, 18½" x 2½" [47 x 6.4cm] (E)
- 2 rectangles, 22½" x 2½" [57.2 x 6.4cm] (F)
- 2 rectangles, 26½" x 2½" [67.3 x 6.4cm] (G)
- 2 rectangles, 30½" x 2½" [77.5 x 6.4cm] (H)
- 2 rectangles, 34½" x 2½" [87.6 x 6.4cm] (I)

After you cut each set of rectangles from each color, organize the rectangles by color and letter.

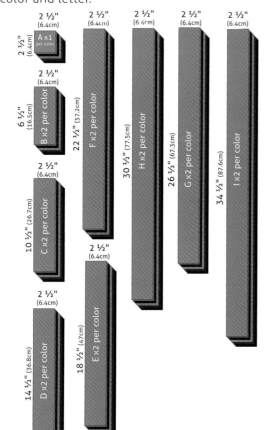

From the background fabrics cut:

7 strips from each color: 2½" (6.4cm) x width of fabric (35 total); for each color, subcut as follows, cutting the longer rectangles first, then cutting the shorter rectangles from the remaining fabric:

- 2 squares, 2½" x 2½" [6.4 x 6.4cm] (A)
- 2 rectangles, 6½" x 2½" [16.5 x 6.4cm] (B)
- 2 rectangles, 10½" x 2½" [26.7 x 6.4cm] (C)
- 2 rectangles, 14½" x 2½" [36.8 x 6.4cm] (D)
- 2 rectangles, 18½" x 2½" [47 x 6.4cm] (E)
- 2 rectangles, 22½" x 2½" [57.2 x 6.4cm] (F)
- 2 rectangles, 26½" x 2½" [67.3 x 6.4cm] (G)
- 2 rectangles, 30½" x 2½" [77.5 x 6.4cm] (H)

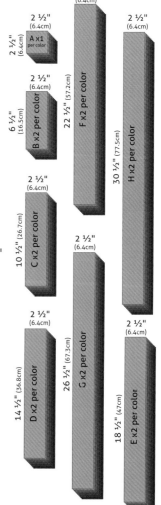

From the sashing fabric cut:

8 strips: 2½" (6.4cm) x width of fabric; subcut into:

- 3 rectangles, 34½" x 2½" [87.6 x 6.4cm] (J)
- 2 rectangles, 16½" x 2½" [41.9 x 6.4cm] (K)

Reserve the remaining 4 strips to use for the horizontal sashing.

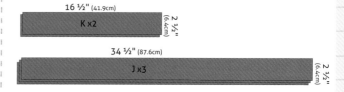

Figure A.

Figure B.

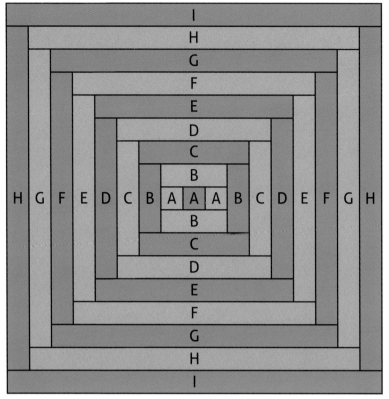

Figure C.

Piecing

Use a scant ¼" (6mm) seam allowance for all seams. Press seam allowances open or to the side as desired; mine are pressed open.

1. Organize the strips from each color by size to make assembly easier. For one block, retrieve a set of rectangles from one focus fabric and one background fabric.

2. Sew two A background squares to each side of an A focus square (Figure A).

3. Add two B background rectangles to the top and bottom (Figure B).

4. Repeat Step 2 with two (B) focus fabric rectangles, sewing them on each side of the existing patchwork. Continue repeating Steps 2 and 3, alternating rounds of increasingly longer background fabric and focus fabric rectangles to complete one block as shown in Figure C. The finished block should measure 34½" x 34½" [87.6 x 87.6cm].

5. Repeat Steps 1–4 four more times with the rest of the focus and background fabrics to make a total of five blocks.

6. Cut two blocks in half down the middle—from I rectangle to I rectangle—to make half-blocks, then trim off a little from the center so that they measure 16½" x 34½" [41.9 x 87.6cm]. Cut one half-block in half again widthwise, and again trim a little bit off so you have two quarter-blocks that measure 16½" x 16½" [41.9 x 41.9cm] (Figure D).

16 ½"
(41.9cm)

16 ½"
(41.9cm)

34 ½"
(87.6cm)

16 ½"
(41.9cm)

Figure D.

Figure E.

Figure F.

7. Using the vertical sashing strips (J and K), connect the full blocks and the half- and quarter-blocks into rows as shown in Figure E.

8. Chain the four strips of horizontal sashing into one long strip, then subcut this into 2 strips both 70½" (179.1cm) long (Figure F).

9. Use the horizontal sashing strips to join the rows.

Finishing

Layer the backing, batting, and quilt top (page 50), baste the layers, quilt as desired (page 48), and bind the raw edges (page 58).

QUILT IT!

It's only fitting that a quilt inspired by the ripples created from throwing pebbles in a pond would be quilted with pebbles! This free-motion pattern is also called cobblestones or ovals, but it's all the same—quilting circles and ovals over and over in close proximity to create the look of a cobblestone street or a pile of pebbles.

Just My Size: **Ripple Quilt**

Would you like to see this quilt made in a different size? Different sizes can be made by constructing more or fewer blocks, then trimming and arranging them according to the desired measurements. Refer to the illustration and chart to find out the block and materials requirements you need, then assemble following the instructions.

Color variations: Would you like to make this quilt in a different color palette? Check out the options here to spark your creativity.

King:
106 ½" x
106 ½"
(270.5 x
270.5cm)

Baby: 34 ½" x 52 ½"
(87.6 x 133.4cm)

Twin:
52 ½" x 88 ½"
(133.4 x 224.8cm)

Queen:
88 ½" x
106 ½"
(224.8 x
270.5cm)

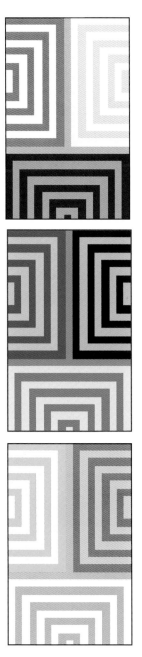

Quilt layout: Use the number of blocks indicated by the illustration and the chart to construct your quilt to size.

Ripple Quilt

	Baby	Twin	Queen	King
Finished size	34½" x 52½" (87.6 x 133.4cm)	52½" x 88½" (133 x 224.8cm)	88½" x 106½" (224.8 x 270.5cm)	106½" x 106½" (270.5 x 270.5cm)
Block configuration:	1 block x 1½ rows (2 blocks)	1½ blocks x 2½ rows (4 blocks)	2½ blocks x 3 rows (8 total)	3 blocks x 3 rows (9 total)
Materials needed				
Coordinating focus fabrics	⅔ yd. (0.7m) each of 2 fabrics	⅔ yd. (0.7m) each of 4 fabrics	⅔ yd. (0.7m) each of 8 fabrics	⅔ yd. (0.7m) each of 9 fabrics
Background fabrics	½ yd. (0.5m) each of 2 fabrics	½ yd. (0.5m) each of 4 fabrics	½ yd. (0.5m) each of 8 fabrics	½ yd. (0.5m) each of 9 fabrics
Sashing fabrics	¼ yd. (0.3m)	½ yd. (0.5m)	1 yd. (1m)	1 yd. (1m)
Batting	43" x 61" (109.2 x 154.9cm)	61" x 97" (154.9 x 246.4cm)	97" x 115" (246.4 x 292.1cm)	115" x 115" (292.1 x 292.1cm)
Backing	1¾ yd. (1.6m) of 60" (152.4cm) wide backing	1¾ yd. (1.6m) of 106" (269.2cm) wide backing	2¾ yd. (2.6m) of 118" (299.7cm) wide backing	3¼ yd. (3m) of 118" (299.7cm) wide backing
Binding	½ yd. (0.5m)	⅔ yd. (0.7m)	1 yd. (1m)	1 yd. (1m)
Blocks				
Focus fabric strips to cut per color:	9 strips: 2½" (6.4cm) x width of fabric	9 strips: 2½" (6.4cm) x width of fabric	9 strips: 2½" (6.4cm) x width of fabric	9 strips: 2½" (6.4cm) x width of fabric
Using the material as efficiently as possible, subcut into:	17 rectangles: • (1) 2½" x 2½" (6.4 x 6.4cm) • (2) 6½" x 2½" (16.5 x 6.4cm) • (2) 10½" x 2½" (26.7 x 6.4cm) • (2) 14½" x 2½" (36.8 x 6.4cm) • (2) 18½" x 2½" (47 x 6.4cm) • (2) 22½" x 2½" (57.2 x 6.4cm) • (2) 26½" x 2½" (67.3 x 6.4cm) • (2) 30½" x 2½" (77.5 x 6.4cm) • (2) 34½" x 2½" (87.6 x 6.4cm)	17 rectangles: • (1) 2½" x 2½" (6.4 x 6.4cm) • (2) 6½" x 2½" (16.5 x 6.4cm) • (2) 10½" x 2½" (26.7 x 6.4cm) • (2) 14½" x 2½" (36.8 x 6.4cm) • (2) 18½" x 2½" (47 x 6.4cm) • (2) 22½" x 2½" (57.2 x 6.4cm) • (2) 26½" x 2½" (67.3 x 6.4cm) • (2) 30½" x 2½" (77.5 x 6.4cm) • (2) 34½" x 2½" (87.6 x 6.4cm)	17 rectangles: • (1) 2½" x 2½" (6.4 x 6.4cm) • (2) 6½" x 2½" (16.5 x 6.4cm) • (2) 10½" x 2½" (26.7 x 6.4cm) • (2) 14½" x 2½" (36.8 x 6.4cm) • (2) 18½" x 2½" (47 x 6.4cm) • (2) 22½" x 2½" (57.2 x 6.4cm) • (2) 26½" x 2½" (67.3 x 6.4cm) • (2) 30½" x 2½" (77.5 x 6.4cm) • (2) 34½" x 2½" (87.6 x 6.4cm)	17 rectangles: • (1) 2½" x 2½" (6.4 x 6.4cm) • (2) 6½" x 2½" (16.5 x 6.4cm) • (2) 10½" x 2½" (26.7 x 6.4cm) • (2) 14½" x 2½" (36.8 x 6.4cm) • (2) 18½" x 2½" (47 x 6.4cm) • (2) 22½" x 2½" (57.2 x 6.4cm) • (2) 26½" x 2½" (67.3 x 6.4cm) • (2) 30½" x 2½" (77.5 x 6.4cm) • (2) 34½" x 2½" (87.6 x 6.4cm)

Ripple Quilt

	Baby	Twin	Queen	King
Background fabric strips to cut per color:	7 strips: 2½" (6.4cm) x width of fabric	7 strips: 2½" (6.4cm) x width of fabric	7 strips: 2½" (6.4cm) x width of fabric	7 strips: 2½" (6.4cm) x width of fabric
Using the material as efficiently as possible, subcut into:	16 rectangles: • (2) 2½" x 2½" (6.4 x 6.4cm) • (2) 6½" x 2½" (16.5 x 6.4cm) • (2) 10½" x 2½" (26.7 x 6.4cm) • (2) 14½" x 2½" (36.8 x 6.4cm) • (2) 18½" x 2½" (47 x 6.4cm) • (2) 22½" x 2½" (57.2 x 6.4cm) • (2) 26½" x 2½" (67.3 x 6.4cm) • (2) 30½" x 2½" (77.5 x 6.4cm)	16 rectangles: • (2) 2½" x 2½" (6.4 x 6.4cm) • (2) 6½" x 2½" (16.5 x 6.4cm) • (2) 10½" x 2½" (26.7 x 6.4cm) • (2) 14½" x 2½" (36.8 x 6.4cm) • (2) 18½" x 2½" (47 x 6.4cm) • (2) 22½" x 2½" (57.2 x 6.4cm) • (2) 26½" x 2½" (67.3 x 6.4cm) • (2) 30½" x 2½" (77.5 x 6.4cm)	16 rectangles: • (2) 2½" x 2½" (6.4 x 6.4cm) • (2) 6½" x 2½" (16.5 x 6.4cm) • (2) 10½" x 2½" (26.7 x 6.4cm) • (2) 14½" x 2½" (36.8 x 6.4cm) • (2) 18½" x 2½" (47 x 6.4cm) • (2) 22½" x 2½" (57.2 x 6.4cm) • (2) 26½" x 2½" (67.3 x 6.4cm) • (2) 30½" x 2½" (77.5 x 6.4cm)	16 rectangles: • (2) 2½" x 2½" (6.4 x 6.4cm) • (2) 6½" x 2½" (16.5 x 6.4cm) • (2) 10½" x 2½" (26.7 x 6.4cm) • (2) 14½" x 2½" (36.8 x 6.4cm) • (2) 18½" x 2½" (47 x 6.4cm) • (2) 22½" x 2½" (57.2 x 6.4cm) • (2) 26½" x 2½" (67.3 x 6.4cm) • (2) 30½" x 2½" (77.5 x 6.4cm)
Sashing				
Sashing fabric strips to cut:	2 strips: 2½" (6.4cm) x width of fabric	6 strips: 2½" (6.4cm) x width of fabric	11 strips: 2½" (6.4cm) x width of fabric	14 strips: 2½" (6.4cm) x width of fabric
Subcut into:	2 rectangles: • 34½" x 2½" (87.6 x 6.4cm)	2 rectangles: • 34½" x 2½" (87.6 x 6.4cm)	6 rectangles: • 34½" x 2½" (87.6 x 6.4cm)	8 rectangles: • 34½" x 2½" (87.6 x 6.4cm)
		1 rectangle: • 16½" x 2½" (41.9 x 6.4cm)		
Horizontal sashing:		Chain 3 strips, then subcut into 2 strips: 2½" x 52½" (6.4 x 133.4cm)	Chain 5 strips, then subcut into 2 strips: 2½" x 88½" (6.4 x 224.8cm)	Chain 6 strips, then subcut into 2 strips: 2½" x 106½" (6.4 x 270.5cm)

Index